THE COUNTRYMAN'S YEAR

Books by
DAVID GRAYSON

RAY STANNARD BAKER (DAVID GRAYSON)
1870-1946

Wrote Ray Stannard Baker on the birth of David Grayson:

"On the whole...I was gloomy about the project; but I was heartened by a letter I soon received. It was written by Lincoln Steffens, an editor and a friend. It was certainly one of the finest apprcciations that ever I received in my life. It was then, and has remained, one of those creative documents in a man's life which give him courage to go on:"

July 25, 1906

My Dear Baker:

Your David Grayson...is beautiful...I was ashamed because I never had realized that there was in you such a sense of beauty, so much fine, philosophic wisdom and, most wonderful of all—serenity...It's a real creative art, Baker, far above and beyond reporting... David Grayson is a great man...

"When I hear people say they have not found
the world, or life so interesting as to be in love
with it I am apt to think they have never . . . seen
with clear vision the world they think so meanly
of, nor anything in it, not even a blade of grass."

—W.H. Hudson

THE
COUNTRYMAN'S
YEAR

By
DAVID GRAYSON

ILLUSTRATIONS BY THOMAS FOGARTY

Second Printing: September, 1986

RENAISSANCE HOUSE PUBLISHERS
A Division of Jende-Hagan, Inc.
541 Oak Street • P.O. Box 177
Frederick, CO 80530

Library of Congress Cataloging in Publication Data

Baker, Ray Stannard, 1870-1946.
    The countryman's year.

    Reprint. Originally published: New York: Doubleday, 1936. With a new foreword.
    1. Baker, Ray Stannard, 1870-1946. 2. Amherst Region (Mass.)--Biography. 3. Country life--Massachusetts--Amherst Region. I. Title.
CT275.B313A28   1985   818'.5203 [B]   85-245

ISBN   0-939650-47-9

FOREWORD TO THE
RENAISSANCE HOUSE EDITION

It often seems, as the old saw has it, that there's nothing new under the sun. And a quick reading of *The Countryman's Year* certainly provides plenty of evidence to support that notion. First published in 1936, this collection of the thoughts and observations of David Grayson (pen name of Pulitzer Prize winning journalist and biographer Ray Stannard Baker) is a veritable treasure-trove of passages that could easily refer to today's late breaking news.

Take, for example, this: "I have moments, in these days of national gloom, financial depression, 'hard times', when I feel it my duty to be sad, or at least cynical—but cannot be—not in spring."

Or this: "The new magic words now sweeping the world are 'Control,' 'Management.' Birth is to be controlled, money managed, industry planned, production regulated. I sat today for a long time listening: I heard no one say anything about self control."

Or another, that could very well have come from the most recent issue of *The Mother Earth News:* "I am firmly convinced that the happiest men I know have their feet—or at least one foot—in the soil. I read the other day an article on the 'back-to-the-land' movement which was far too sanguine. Country life is not to be taken by storm, nor happiness acquired by moving into a farmhouse. And yet I know many instances in which the world has been changed for human beings by going to live in a garden, or by cultivating a few rods or acres of land as part of a life occupied with other things. I have in mind a spinster saved by three flowerpots—but that is a story I will tell some other time."

Or one more, that might have come to your mind, or mine, this very morning: "One of the things that irritates me extremely—in short makes me angry—is the insulting disregard, common in this country, of natural beauty. Piles of old tin cans and rubbish dumped in a beautiful roadside brook—I know of such a case—motorcars left to rust in open meadows—fir trees needlessly hacked to make way for eyesore telephone poles—all billboards whatsoever! These things are evidences of our lack of civilization."

However, there's another truth to be gained from reading *The Countryman's Year,* a truth that often has a lot more value than the somewhat comforting (though often frustrating) idea that the world around us doesn't change. Because a more careful reading of this book shows us that there *is* something new under the sun— something that can be pleasing, strengthening, and, I might as well say it, downright inspiring. That something is the always unique way that the minds and hearts of intelligent and sensitive men and women react to the goings-on of this ever-changing and seemingly changeless world.

In this slim book, David Grayson gives us the opportunity to *share* the workings of one such mind, one such heart. And I, for one, am very grateful to have had the chance.

Bruce Woods, Editor *The Mother Earth News*

PUBLISHER'S PREFACE

The Countryman's Year was rediscovered just as David Grayson would have liked it—on a shelf of commonplace books in a country house in a small Maine village. Its worn, water-stained binding and rather musty smell gave it the air of its companion volumes on the shelf: authors whose time had come and gone...interesting, perhaps, as literature of another era, but nothing very relevant to today.

The inscription on the endsheet read:

> *Your Birthday Book, John Dear,*
> *May 1937 bring you a bumper crop—garden,*
> *friends and happiness...*
>
> *Elsie*

The inscription beckoned on to the first page: April of The Countryman's Year "where," the author decided, "it would be best to break into the magic circle of the seasons." And the pages kept beckoning on, through each month of The Countryman's Year. Despite its common appearance, its relatively unknown author and its 50-year-old copyright, it was undeniably a book for today's readers...because David Grayson's thoughts and observations are timeless, pertinent, and just a joy to read. Wanting immediately to share *The Countryman's Year,* we scoured dozens of used book shops, but turned up not a single copy. The die was cast to republish David Grayson.

Through the helpful staff at the copyright office in Washington, we first discovered that David Grayson was actually the pen name of Pulitzer Prize winning journalist Ray Stannard Baker. Good fortune brought us in touch with the heirs of Mr. Baker who were delighted to have his work republished and most cooperative throughout the many copyright entanglements. After months of legal roadblocks and seeming dead ends, Attorney Ellen Kozak, a copyright specialist, wrote us with the good news that the way was cleared to once again put David Grayson into print. Bruce Woods, editor of *The Mother Earth News* shared our enthusiasm for the book and his support in writing a Foreword to the RENAISSANCE HOUSE edition has reinforced our belief that the thoughts of a common man 50 years ago can be most relevant and inspiring today. We hope that you, too, share this enthusiasm.

FOREWORD

Many years ago I came to the hillside in the town of Amherst where I now live. I bought a few acres of land and built a house. I planted trees and cultivated my garden. I kept bees. I made good friends among my neighbors. Here I have known the best, I think, that comes to any man—times of sight that is also insight.

Although my life, as I said in an earlier book called *Adventures in Contentment,* has been "much occupied with other employment," I have liked these experiences in the country better than anything else that ever I knew, and have written about them, day by day, in many small notebooks, thus enlarging my life by expressing it. I have also put down in my notes comments upon books I read, people I met and, above all, the things I meditated upon as I went about doing the quiet work of my land, my orchard and my bees. Sometimes I have thought: give me time enough here in this place and I will surely make a beautiful thing.

Some few of these notes I have now copied out, literally as written month by month through the countryman's year. I have always liked best books that have been lived before being written. It is not experience alone that makes a man interesting to himself or to his neighbors—I once saw an ass looking at Rome—but the afterthoughts and transmutations of experience.

At first I thought I would call these chapters *The Quiet Way,* since they deal with so many quiet and simple things, and are in no way outwardly exciting, but I decided finally upon a title more exactly descriptive: *The Countryman's Year.*

I give you here the best I have seen and heard in my brief passage through this arc of space, this instant of time. It is as far as I have gone at present: at present I have thought no further. I live here and am quiet.

DAVID GRAYSON

CONTENTS

APRIL

IN THE COUNTRYMAN'S YEAR

"After you have exhausted what there is in business, politics, conviviality, love, and so on—have found that none of these finally satisfy, or permanently wear—what remains? Nature remains: to bring out from their torpid recesses the affinities of a man or woman with the open air—the sun by day and the stars of heaven by night."
WALT WHITMAN in *Specimen Days.*

CHAPTER I

APRIL IN THE COUNTRYMAN'S YEAR

I HAD some doubt, in beginning this book, where it would be best to break into the magic circle of the seasons, whether at the conventional entrance, in January, or at the first faint intimacies of the awakening of spring. In the old calendars the New Year began with the vernal equinox in March, according to the logic of the sun and the moon and the stars, but restless human beings will be

forever trying to vote their own way; and
when the Gregorian calendar was adopted in
America in the year 1752 New Year's Day
was changed from March 25 to January 1.

As a matter of fact, the year begins for the
true countryman at the moment when he puts
his foot down into the soil of his own land.
Once in my life I began in the heyday of
summer, the robust middle age of the year;
and once, returning to my own hillside like
some lost prodigal from the husks of a far
country, I began it at the time of the apple
picking and the cider making in October. I
cannot see that it was not as good at one time
as another: but since this is a narrative of a
normal year I shall begin with the first shy
touches of spring that come to our New England hills.

APRIL 1. Endless winter, raw and cold. Spring
comes reluctantly. Old icy drifts still cling
to the hillside, and in our garden there are
patches of rotten snow north of the pines. We
had a few days of fine weather in March
when I was able to finish the pruning of my
apple trees, but for the most part now for
many days we have been living in a gray and

sodden world wherein the key virtue is endurance. I saw today one of my Polish neighbors tramping disconsolately across his field, no doubt wondering when he can get his plow down into the soil and plant his onions.

APRIL 2. Worse and worse. A great snowstorm, a blizzard almost, is raging across the country. The earth looks like the dead of winter, as though the year had lost its way in the storm and turned backward. I have been hard at work all day at my desk. If I have lived in what Emerson calls the "tumultuous privacy of the storm," at least I have been uninterrupted, which is a blessing in itself.

This evening we had a bright blaze on our hearth and sat near it—with what comfort! —listening to the wind complaining at the windows and rattling at the doorways. I have been reading with keen pleasure—really rereading—a book by John Jay Chapman, wherein there is much pointed criticism of both life and literature. "The closer you examine honesty and intellect," says he, "the more clearly they appear to be the same thing."

APRIL 4. A blessed touch of spring in the air. Last night it rained, quietly, softly, all night long, and this morning the earth seems new-born, the landscape wrapped in a soft mist through which the sun comes shyly stealing as though to lift the veil of a virgin earth. There are wide open spaces in the fields, bare, brown, inviting, and subdued bird notes; and in the distance across Farley's farm, I can hear the cattle calling.

The birds are coming! Besides many that remain here during the winter, a pair of pheasants, a pair of marsh hawks, crows in great numbers, blackbirds and chickadees, I have seen robins, jays and song sparrows. I stood today for a long time watching a bird I think I never saw here before, brown above, with mottled breast and a longish red tail. "It is of the thrushes," I said, yet it did not look large enough. It seemed too large for a sparrow. It did not sing, but there was a happy little "chip, chip, chip" as it ran along the branch of a maple tree. Coming home I found him in my infallible book—a fox sparrow, not common here. I have also had delight recently in watching the black-capped chickadees— surely among the delightfulest of birds. I wish

I had a deeper and more special knowledge of birds and bird life. If only I had time! One life does not begin to satisfy a man's curiosity: it turns only the first page of the book of wonders. I like to plan what I shall do with my future lives, one after another, if ever I get them. One of the first, after this, I shall devote largely to birds and bees.

On my return across the fields I tested, oddly, the capacities of this town. I met farmer K—— leading his little bright Jersey cow, and fell to talking with him. When I asked him the age of his Jersey he pushed back the hair around its horns and counted the rings and then gave me an eloquent lecture on telling the age of cows and the certainty of it compared with judging the age of horses by their teeth. Teeth could be filed. This brought him to stirring episodes in the life of a black mare named Nancy whose teeth did not exactly meet, and further remarks regarding a former Jersey cow that had five teats, but one would not milk. Coming back I met Professor T——, for I live in the periphery of a college, and found him hot upon the Einstein theory. I told him I had read some chapters of Slosson's small book on the subject to my complete obfuscation, whereat he was off. He came home with me and sat by my fire while we discussed mighty things, most of which I did not fully understand. I reflected, however, on the resources of a neighborhood that in one afternoon could unfold the lore of Jersey cows and the Einstein theory.

APRIL 6. A high windy day, with sunshine and the blue jays calling. Snowdrops in bloom, first of all, and the bees active, finding something, I think, among the chickweed buds. But the year has not yet come alive.

Looking over a group of old letters from among the necessary documents of my task, I reflect upon what a world of anxiety and pain there is among human beings over troubles that never happen!

APRIL 12. I grafted one of my huge young Wolf River apple trees to Roxbury Russets on one side and Palmer Greenings on the other. It was cold and misty, and I had trouble with the wax. Spring hesitates.

APRIL 13. Snow is still visible in the hills, but the air is delightfully warm and sunny: my bees are bringing in pollen. The weather being uncertain, I have had a week of more or less uninterrupted labor at my desk.

So now, accept the dull interludes. Know that the spirit also must rest. If one burned constantly, nothing would remain but gray ash. Where goes the creative spark? Yesterday I was master of my world: I rode the wind; I touched the stars; almost I caught the blinding glory of God; but today I am a clod. I am a clod. Well—I accept also my clod-hood. Such days I work in the soil, or tramp in the fields, as I did today: I court weariness of body and patience of spirit.

APRIL 14. Up at six and worked all day in my garden and orchard. In the early morning the ground was crusted with frost, and the air was sharp and cool, though of a crystal brightness. I raised the incense of burning brush to the Most High, and all day long I listened for the undertones of that harmony which must be in this universe, if only a man might tune his soul to the hearing of it. Too short such days as these, and the joy of them.

APRIL 15. Blessed quiet, thinking and working. The yellow lace of the forsythia now ornaments the bosom of spring, and there are pendants, gay blossoms of poplar and coral gems of the soft maple, in her hair, and she sings, a bluebird, at my study window.

The crocuses and snowdrops are in bloom.

I am trying to set up a rule: to work at my desk in the forenoon, in my garden in the afternoon.

APRIL 16. Heavy wet snow, like winter again. All the trees are covered, the hemlock branches borne down by it, fine to see. Our old New Englanders who believe religiously in the law of compensation expected it; we are being paid for the bright warm days of last week. Some kind of misery must of necessity follow every real moment of joy.

I saw a man today who has achieved serenity, and knew he had accepted himself as a failure and gone about his business.

APRIL 18. It is the time of the false spring, the time of the foretokening bloom of the elms, red maples, poplars and willows: blossoms that will soon be falling and give us

again a barren remembrance of winter. I love
well this moment of the spring: the russets
and browns of the marshes, and the new ruddy
look of the hillsides. The edges of the fields
are coming green: yesterday in the bare soil
under the sumacs in our garden I found hya-
cinths in bloom. The first stirrings of new
life! Why is it, as we grow older, that these
moments of spring should be, yearly, more
wistfully beautiful?

The comfort and beauty of common things:
how deep it is in the blood of us! I have been
working hard physically in my garden and
orchard this spring. What agreeable weariness it brings: what keen-set hunger! What
drafts of blessed sleep! How all the senses are
sharpened to awareness, especially the sense
of smell. I walked up across the fields from
Farley's farm yesterday, just at noon, and had
keenly at least twenty different odors of the
bare fields, the blossoming hedges, the cattle,
the marshy earth, the fertilizer that Steve is
spreading on my field—and finally, as I came
in at my own doorway, the ambrosia of broil-
ing ham, newly cooked in the kitchen. No one
knows who does not know!

It seems to me I never enjoyed all these things more than I have this year.

When I go to Boston or New York I begin to worry about the state of the nation—and civilization generally. So much unrest, such unreason, such violence, such utter folly! But when I come home to my own hills and get down to work among these everyday, normal people, I am reassured. So many millions there are leading their steady quiet lives, absorbed in the common processes of existence: working, eating, sleeping, hoping, struggling, failing, loving. All their thinking seems somehow to have its roots in the soil. What they do and are and feel is rarely reported in any newspaper or set down in any book: so that the world judges its civilization not by its preponderant normality but by its "news," its sensations and abnormalities. I never come home to my hillside without a renewed sense of the assured soundness and continuity of life. Oh, I know that great changes are certain to come—has there ever yet been anything but change?—but they will be slow, slow. If they are genuine changes, not mere superficial symbols, they will be slow.

I have had working here this spring a plowman named W——. He is about thirty-five years old, and has a fine big team of horses, a roan and a black. He has had a common school education, is married, and has two bright children in our school. Just as a human being, he is well worth looking at, not tall or large, but robust, with tremendous muscular shoulders. He can plow steadily all day in heavy land and whistle as he goes up the hill on his way home at night. He has a "side-hill" or swivel plow of the largest size. A side-hill plow is set on a hinge and is thrown over at the end of each furrow so that the earth is all turned in one direction and the plowing is straight back and forth across the field: a practice especially adapted to these uneven and hilly New England farms. But the labor required, especially in sod land, is prodigious. The entire plow has to be lifted out of the earth with any moist soil that clings to it, the share has to be swung or kicked over until it catches on the other side, and then the whole plow has to be pulled backward for the start of a new furrow. I have tried it my-self and know what a cruel backbreaker it is.

W—— wears a blue denim shirt and stout suspenders with the word "Police" on the buckle, and smokes a short pipe of strong tobacco. He is proud of his big team: has the harness straps trimmed up with colored rings, and there are little rosettes on the bridles, and all the harness gleams with recent rubbing. He knows to the uttermost the peculiarities of each animal, what he will do in emergencies, how much he will stand, and his full history and value. I like to go out at the nooning when he is sitting with his back against the cart seat on the shady side of the wagon, legs spread out, and dinner pail between his knees, and talk with him. He *likes* plowing and is proud of his prowess. He has the true satisfaction in what he is doing that makes for human happiness. I have probed him for discontents. Yes, he is discontented, if you probe him for it—what human being is not, especially what farmer?—but usually he is too busy: and certainly too little self-conscious.

Judgments upon "society" are so often passed by writers who do not really know or feel normal people. They judge neighbors like mine as though each were a self-conscious, self-analyzing, egotistical human being like themselves. They are dependent for sensation upon the abnormalities, the tragedies, the ignorances—all of which are there, as everywhere—but they do not see the man *in proportion:* his normal life as a worker, the simple interests and joys, the consoling vanity he has in the thing he is doing. We commonly underestimate the immense and solid satisfaction, the comfort, countrymen get out of the homeliest facts of life: eating, sleeping, working, resting, playing, loving—smoking! Currying horses, discussing cows, dogs, fertilizers, seeds; driving automobiles, tinkering farm machinery, spraying trees, building a new back porch, planting a vine, putting up a trellis; reading the newspaper, listening to the radio. I could name a thousand things more!

APRIL 20. My work hangs heavy. My mind will not stay in my study but will be flying away to the fields and the hills. In the midst of the dry documents of my daily labor I think suddenly, and with a wave of longing, of my garden starting into life, the buds swelling on the orchard trees, the bees flying— and I not there to see. I am a sad weakling who would yield to what he loves. My little walks these mornings before I sit down to work are a pure delight.

Let them have their California. I choose my own hillside here in New England. Their own flamboyant California: my own reticent New England: no beauty wholesale!

By writing I enjoy life twice: and that is necessary, since life is so short. I do not bother at all to write of anything that does not interest me. I wait until my curiosity or my fondness boils up to the writing point. The other day I chanced upon one of Arthur Waley's collections of old Chinese poems wherein I found one by Po Chü-i, written over a thousand years ago, which seems to me to express exactly the mood I mean:

"Each time that I look at a fine landscape:
Each time that I meet a loved friend,
I raise my voice and recite a stanza of poetry
And am glad as though a God had crossed
* my path."*

APRIL 22. After three warm days everything is starting at once. In the garden the forsythia is coming into glowing bloom: and the daffodils: it is the yellow of the year. Steve has been spreading manure: also getting a small plot of land ready for the early vegetables.

I have been taking a number of colonies of my bees out of their winter boxes. I have had them safe packed in shavings and old leaves, and they have wintered perfectly. Every colony is alive and vigorous. I put on my veil and gloves and went through Number 5 as a test and found it in excellent condition, full of bees, new worker brood and eggs, and as yet no queen cells and no drones. Plenty of old honey is left over, and some new is being brought in, from what source it is difficult to say. It is a pleasure to be handling the bees again. I have been at it now every spring for more than twenty years and find my interest unabated.

I was rereading this evening Masefield's invaluable little book on Shakespeare: "The great poets have agreed that anything that distorts the mental vision, anything thought of too much, is a danger to us. . . . Reality, however obtained, is the only cure for obsession."

And here he strikes a note of deep penetration: "One of the truths of the play [*Richard the Third*] is a very sad one, that being certain is in itself a kind of sin, sure to be avenged by life."

APRIL 23. I drove to the mill at North Amherst with a small load of corn to grind. The plowman is abroad in all the land, and I saw several farmers setting up their tobacco frames.

The old mill stands at the edge of a little valley, the stream from which has been led around the hillside in a canal so ancient that the banks are grown up to sturdy trees. I like to watch the clear water, coming from the haunts of trout and of deer, plunging into the penstock above the water wheel. The old gray millstones, shipped from France a century or more ago and brought overland by ox teams all of a hundred and fifty miles from New London, are still in good condition. The grandfather of the present owner built the canal and the sluice and the wooden mill, which is now old and gray, with green wet moss covering all the north side where the spray wets it. When the valley was still new and wild, and George III was King of Eng-

land, the virgin soil grew wheat, which the
miller ground into coarse gray flour. Today
not a bushel of wheat is grown in all our valley, but the farmers still bring in their rye
for the miller to grind, and they themselves
afterwards sift it. And I bring my corn. Most
of the business is now corn meal, ground for
poultry feed.

We emptied the bags into the iron crushing
mill, cogged with great blunt teeth, which
tore the corn, cobs and all, into bits. It was
then conveyed through the chute to the stones
beyond, and the miller and I stood with hands
in the down-falling meal to make sure that
the appropriate fineness had been reached.

Looking about, I liked the ancient dusty
look of the old rafters, I liked the odor of
the grinding meal, I liked to hear the rush
of water in the penstock, the jar of the wheel,
the busy whir of the stones.

The miller hooked my bags one after another to the chute and, as they were filled,
busily shook them down, deftly folded in the
top, tied them up, and set them on the scales.

Your miller is a true talking worker: the
kind I enjoy. He can watch his mill, tend the
flow of the grist, and yet find time for the great

and good talk of the neighborhood—the problems of the onion growers, the tobacco acreage, the earliness of the spring, the perennial talk among the old Yankee stock of the invasion of Polish farmers.

"Did ye hear that a Pole has come into the street and bought the old H—— farm? What do ye think o' that! Next thing ye know, they'll have all the valley."

APRIL 24. Everywhere I go I hear people groaning over the hard times—financial loss, profitless business, falling wages. But when I walk down through my meadow and along the old road into the woods and by the brook, I find no depression. The brown fields lie there waiting, expectant; the sun shines; the water glistens; the birds sing.

I was reminded today, as so often before, of the continuity and permanence of nature. All the sights I saw, the sounds I heard, came in upon me as in every spring I ever knew before. And in every spring of future years, whether I am here or not, there will be the same glow of red maples in the marsh, the same rusty mist of elms, the same blooming daffodils, the same robins in wide, green

meadows, and flashing bluebirds in old fence
corners. All the sweet repetition of the symphony of spring.

Life is brief, and times, they say, are hard:
a nation anxious and alarmed: all men fearful
of disaster—this they say—and yet all these
things I saw this morning, as I walked, and
returned newly assured.

And yet what a time it truly is—with so
many people leaning on the town, so many
towns leaning on the state, so many states leaning on the nation—and the nation leaning on
the President! Let the people stand on their
own legs, let the towns stand, and the states
stand, and the nation stand. The President is a
weak reed. How long can the President stand
up, with all the people leaning on him?

"A man," says Marcus Aurelius, "must
stand erect, not be kept erect by others."

APRIL 26. This contrary New England spring!
Hard frost last night: glorious clear summer
sunshine this morning. I am busy all my spare
time in the garden and with the bees. Setting
out a number of new peach trees to replace
weakened old ones. Trying to raise peaches

in this northern climate is a perfect example of the way in which hope springs eternal in the human breast: or else it is the kind of sanguine madness that attacks the countryman in spring. I have been trying to raise peaches on this hillside for twenty-three years and have not had more than three or four respectable crops. Twice mature trees have been killed by frosts, and often all the buds have been blasted. And yet we go on year after year! I am also preparing for a new asparagus bed to take the place of one long ago worn out. Steve and I gave the apple trees the delayed dormant spray.

"I think," says Thoreau (in the second chapter of *Walden,* I was reading today), "that the richest vein is somewhere hereabouts."

It is true: people do not change essentially —except in learning to let out all they have. There is an immense opportunity, even for the old, to be *more* of what they are. What most human beings lack is not endowment, but intensity of endowment.

APRIL 28. Spring is here with a rush after two fine warm days. It was with difficulty

I lived up to my rule and remained at my desk all the forenoon. We finished spraying the apple orchard, and in a warm spot south of the pines I put in a few rows of early garden: smooth peas, spinach, lettuce, carrots. I have been going through the bee colonies to make sure of their condition, especially the vigor of the queens. I have begun my yearly card record of the colonies in which I keep a careful report, with dates, of each examination. Some beekeepers I know, who delight in thinking of themselves as "practical," laugh at my "bookkeeping," but I find it the only satisfactory method. I know of no other way to be sure of controlled swarming: and unless swarming is controlled, there is likely to be little surplus honey to reward the keeper for his pains.

I was not here at the naming of the birds, or the flowers, or the hills. I wish I had been. Naming beautiful things—is that not the true office, as it is the joy, of the poet? And there has been so much naming when poets were not there, when dull souls could find no word to describe a flame of a bird except to say that it was red. Or to traduce one of the loveliest of our songsters, a bird, moreover, of rare charm of personality, by fastening upon it a name which suggests only its resemblance to a cat. "Catbird!" Heaven-sent warbler! First cousin to the mockingbird and quite as fine a singer. And why all the dull catalogue—"bluebird," "blackbird," "cowbird"?

But if dull souls were there at the naming, so, also, were the poets. What could be finer than "bobolink," "oriole," "flicker"? "Robin" and "lark" are well enough, but the names take their beauty from the birds and do not in themselves glorify the birds or interpret them. "Crow" is good, and especially "hawk." I think the name "hawk" whenever I see the swift, the bold, the predatory bird.

I do not like locality names: "Maryland yellow-throat" for a bird whose "witchery, witchery" is as bewitching on my hillside as ever it was in Maryland. And so "Kentucky cardinal" for a flame of life and a joy of song known throughout half the continent—known even here in these northern places. "Whip-poorwill," perfect! "Sparrow," a name I love, whether the word or the bird, or both, I cannot say. It may be that I am moved by those lines I heard so often when as a shy boy I sat on the hard wooden bench of the hard, hard church of my youth and listened to the rolling words of the Scotch preacher:

"I am like a pelican of the wilderness: I am like an owl of the desert.

"I watch, and am as a sparrow alone upon the housetop."

"A sparrow alone upon the housetop." I shall never forget the *feeling* of those words, hearing in afteryears the sparrow at noon, singing. I shall be homesick for it to the time of the dimness of my eyes and the dullness of my ears, when names no longer thrill me, nor the birds that flash in the sunshine and fill my world with song.

"What's doing, that has life: what's done is dead."

What a blessed anodyne these days is work —hard physical work. I came in last night after having planted potatoes and set out strawberry plants until my legs ached. I came in so tired that I stumbled into bed and fell at once into a deep sleep—a deep, blessed sleep —and awakened this morning with the sound

of rain in the gutters and a vast sense of renewal.

SUNDAY. In the woods. How pleasant this
Sunday morning to sit in the sun. I have
worked hard all the week: and have now a
blessed moment of rest. I left the wind on the
shoulder of Mount Warner and came here to
a little valley I know among the trees: and
sit now with my back to the master pine of
them all. I can hear the wind, like distant
surf, rolling in the forest tops, but where I sit
it is still and warm: and all the air pungent
with the smell of pine needles. The crows are
nesting in their rookery. I can hear their intimate conversation, for I came so quietly
through the wood that I did not set them, as
usual, to clanging with alarm. Some lesser
bird notes are audible, and afar off in the
fields, the strident whistling of a woodchuck.
How still it all is. Spring seems truly here at
last. As I came by the brook and across the
marshes I saw that the willows were yellow
with bloom and full of bees.

I have been wondering how much of my
deep feeling for this moment of the spring is
due to the experiences of my boyhood in the

North, and the Indian guides and woodsmen I sometimes cruised or camped with: who taught me a respect which grew into deep love for such wilderness places. I had a rich youth! Would I love it all so much if it were new and strange to me? Would it seem so much like home? For almost all the common things here about me, plant and animal and insect, I know familiarly by name, something of the why and how of them, something of the uses for them. They are like old friends, always the same, without fickleness. Every sound, sight, odor comes in upon me this morning with new-old intimacy, blessing the soul.

Or am I wrong? Is this thrill of familiarity older far than the Indians and the woodsmen of my youth? Is it not deep-tinctured in the very blood of me, out of generations of pioneering ancestors, always marching westward toward the setting sun, always breaking the virgin soil, always rejoicing when, in that cold land, spring at last unlocked the fastnesses of winter and gave them again the freedom of the hills? For there is something deep in our race that turns us to the wilderness in spring, seeking new things, a new life, a new home.

Or am I still wrong? Is this love of wide fields, woods, and the secret hills in the spring deeper even than the blood of my pioneering ancestors? Deep, deep, in the race it seems to stir: deeper than civilization, deeper far than any superficial memory or experience. During what endless generations, thousands of years, before man was really man, has our stock crept out of the miserable caves and hovels of winter to rest and sweeten themselves in just such warm and sunny hollows of the hills as this in which I am now resting —and with what nameless joy! The same birches and hemlocks were growing here: the same soothing wind surf moved in their tops: the same birds were in the branches—this million years. Oh, it is deep in us, this love of the open air and the trees and the marshes in spring. It is native to our breed: congenial to the blood of us.

—Well, I have somehow aroused the rookery. An old watchful crow, looking down into the depths of the wood where I sit, as into the luminous water of some subtler ocean, thinks he has spied an enemy (little he knows!), and with three startled cries he has set the entire army of crows to clanging. I shall move on

and let the people of the woods enjoy their
Sunday quiet—-

"The dear lone lands, untroubled of men,
  Where no voice sounds, and amid the shad-
    owy green
  The little things of the woodland live un-
    seen."

APRIL 30. I bought several dozen cabbage
plants from Johnson, and we set them in the
open garden. It is early yet, but cabbages will
stand a considerable frost. We have planted
four long rows of Cobbler potatoes. I am so
much interested in the garden and orchard
these days—to say nothing of my bees—that I
find it difficult to keep at my desk, according
to my rule, for the entire forenoon.

I am firmly convinced that the happiest
men I know have their feet—or at least one
foot—in the soil. I read the other day an article on the "back-to-the-land" movement which
was far too sanguine. Country life is not to
be taken by storm: nor happiness acquired
by moving into a farmhouse. And yet I know
many instances in which the world has been
changed for human beings by going to live in

a garden, or by cultivating a few rods or acres of land as a part of a life occupied with other things. I have in mind a spinster saved by three flowerpots—but that is a story I shall tell some other time.

—Just after writing these comments I ran across a delicious passage in Montaigne which points what I have said. Even an emperor could find enlargement in a garden! When Diocletian, after resigning his crown, was called back by the "urgent necessitie of publike affaires," he said—according to Montaigne:

"You would never undertake to perswade me to that [to return] had you but seene the goodly rankes of trees which myselfe have planted in mine Orchard, or the faire muske-melons I have set in my garden."

Once a man, even an emperor, has felt the lure, he never quite recovers from it. The "goodly rankes of trees in mine Orchard," the "faire muske-melons in my garden"—how well I know such delights!

MAY

IN THE COUNTRYMAN'S YEAR

" 'Tis a rugged road, more so than it seems, to follow a pace so rambling and uncertain as that of the soul . . . to choose and lay hold of so many little nimble motions."—MONTAIGNE.

CHAPTER II

MAY IN THE COUNTRYMAN'S YEAR

MAY 2. First peach blossoms. It is the time of the year when the apple orchard, not yet in bloom, is a glory of misty grays and greens of the new foliage. I have been going through the remainder of my bee colonies. Three of them are in the strongest condition this spring —in spite of the hard winter—that ever I knew, full of brood, with enough new honey to carry along. I found a few drones already hatched out, but no queen cells. It is a pleasure to see them in such good order.

Our business is profitable this spring, our investments, in spite of unemployment and crashes in the stock market, are highly successful. We have two green cottages with overhanging eaves and fine porches to rest upon, and both are early rented and well occupied by safe and agreeable tenants, one a family of wrens, the other bluebirds.

A sense of limited days comes upon me. I have so much left to see, and hear, and smell, and touch: so much to think and to feel: my days are too few and too short.

MAY 3. I have been watching my plowman plowing in the cool, sunny, moist spring morning. I have been watching him with admiration and envy. To be out at daybreak with a great farm wagon, a fine team of horses, a plow, a harrow: to be stout, ruddy, forthright! He turns in the green manure (winter rye), kicking aside the furrows that are too stiff to lie down. He pulls his plow out on the grass at the end of the furrow, throwing his shoulder against the reins to bring the team around.

"Get over there: goddam you, Molly!" says he. "You would turn if you didn't have to, damn you."

Molly turns obediently. She does not mind being sworn at. It is the common plow language, nor does the plowman know that he is profane, nor is he angry, nor is he even impatient. It is part of the familiar process.

"Fine land," says he. "She turns over fine. That rye 'll make good corn."

So he plows the long furrows, the sun rises higher, and the blackbirds, spying the new-turned land, come down on the black earth to look for worms. They waddle as they walk and exchange profane comments and eye the horses and the plowman with suspicion.

I am envious of it all. To turn the earth! To be young and strong! To hold so perfectly in control two great horses! To work to weariness, to go home with an appetite that the gods might envy, to sleep like any child!

It is one of the tragedies of our times that so many of us think our rebellious thoughts in private, leading two lives. If only we could have been disgraced, ostracized, defeated, we might have dared.

How few of us are as brave as our dreams!

MAY 6. An event! I saw the first brown thrush of the year.

I brought in asparagus and rhubarb, and we had them for supper: nothing choicer than these first flavors of the garden.

In the presence of nature, as of the works of men, many there are who have only statistical wonder: a taller tree, a deeper gorge, a bigger lake, somewhere else.

Reading a life of Goethe. He was a morning worker—"skimming the cream off the day and using the rest of the time for cheese making." An excellent system.

I stopped today to talk with S——, Polish onion grower, at the edge of his field. He is ignorant and wise. Certain subjects one can talk about with people anywhere upon terms of equality—that is, upon death and birth and love and work, which, after all, are the principal subjects of all conversations upon this planet. S—— said to me that "a man can pay his way out of almost any trouble but death."

I have had this day a strange sense of unexplained well-being.

MAY 9. The apple trees are in full bloom: a gorgeous show: a banquet for the bees. Our orchard never looked finer.

An old, deformed, diseased apple tree on the border of a near-by field, which bears in the fall only stunted, wormy, or scabby fruit, yet blossoms as riotously in May as any tree in my groomed orchard. It will have its day of beauty.

Reading as my evening bed book Hudson's *Far Away and Long Ago*—a rare delight. Why haven't I had it before? Hudson has the charm of a kind of serene melancholy: of happiness in spite of hopelessness.

"Praised be my Lord for our mother the Earth, the which doth sustain us and keep us, and bringeth forth divers fruits, and flowers of many colors, and grass."

Lifting off thought after thought I know well where my joy is: in things still and scenes quiet, in days like these in May in our own valley, in my bees, in my orchard, in the thrushes and catbirds I hear singing, in the flash of a bluebird's wing. These I love: these quiet my soul.

MAY 12. I have to confess, with whatever contrition, that often during these May mornings, sitting at my laborious desk, in my stuffy study, I long for an interruption—almost any interruption except the postman—that will take me out of doors. I know the immorality of it: it offends the rule I have solemnly adopted: it wastes my precious and all too limited time for my work in this world, but how I long to be tempted!

This morning I had the most delightful of interruptions. Steve came to the door to tell me that the bees were swarming. I rushed to the doorway, and there, in the sunny air above the hives, I saw a great cloud of bees filling all the garden with the music of their bassoon. The first of the year! Already they were gathering above one of the Baldwin apple trees, and there I knew they were preparing to light.

I will not here describe the hiving of the

swarm—no one touches my bees but me—but merely emphasize the fact that this was a necessary interruption, and wholly delightful, in spite of the fact that May swarms are often regarded as an evidence of poor beekeeping.

I find keen pleasure in all the minute, careful, deft processes, the infinite problems, presented by the apiary. I lie awake sometimes at night thinking of the unending marvels of the bee civilization—studied by mankind for two thousand years, still not understood. They have secrets, the bees: senses, gifts, we do not know. Among the Quakers there is a spiritual process of coming to communal agreement, after silence, without argument, and without voting on the question involved. (A vote, at best, is a crude confession of inability to reach a decision based upon complete conviction: it is a method of forcing a balance.) Some such secret process of communal decision exists among the bees. One who has handled them long and knows them well comes to sense the moment—and to wait for it as the Quakers wait—but, strain as he will, pry with wonder and thought into the secret of it, he remains baffled by the swift decisiveness with which a swarm of thirty or fifty thousand bees will act as a unit, apparently without consultation or perceptible communication. There is indeed a language of the swarm, the timbre of its humming (perhaps) of which the beeman comes to know a syllable or two, as one traveling in Persia learns the word for "bread." But how a swarm, like the one I hived this morning, hanging out on the branch of an apple tree, knows when or where to fly for a new home, who can tell? A hundred, perhaps a thousand, scouts have gone out through the wide countryside to look for a suitable place and are constantly returning with their reports. How is the news communicated? How do the fifty thousand bees decide which report to accept, what scout to follow? Answer that, my little wise man! When the swarm rises after hanging for an hour or even a day—unless you yourself, acting the part of demigod, have hived them—they swirl about, a dark, swift, roaring cloud in the air, and then make a "beeline" across the valley or up the hill, straight to the spot chosen. It is true that they sometimes find the place unsuitable and rest again in a tree or on a fence post to send out new scouts (do they in such cases abuse the culprit scout with sarcastic bee editorials, as men might do?), but that in no way alters the marvel.

I like all these quiet, interesting processes. At this time of year one need scarcely wear a veil or gloves if he knows how to go about the delicate business of handling the bees, if he observes, with courtesy and gentleness, and the slow thoroughness which the scientist cultivates, the manners and customs of this ancient democracy of the bee people. I know of no other occupation more soothing to spirits plagued by the problems of living: there is salvation to minds distraught and souls unstrung in these quiet and simple processes of the hands.

And there is another aspect of such employment, of the adventures of which I could write an entire book. Any genuine simple process which a man loves, of which he has made himself a master, inevitably leads to interesting and genuine human contacts. I could tell of many a beekeeper I have met in my travels, sometimes uncultivated men, men not rich in goods, and found them full of curious knowledge, or of true-won wisdom concerning the way to live endurably in a crowded world. A man is best judged not by his ignorance but by his knowledge, and there is almost no man living from whom there is not something to be learned—if we know how to get at it. There are in reality no classes, no human pigeonholes—there are only diverse and strange and incredibly interesting individual human beings, each set like a star in a vast and roomy universe. If only we were willing to handle men with the courtesy of spirit, the respect for variant manners, with which we handle the bees, half the woes of the world, I think, would disappear. But there is so much trampling roughshod through the sensitive world of human personality!

Once I went out, hotly, eagerly, to seek other men, thinking they had things I wanted: now I sit quiet here and men seek me, thinking I have things they want.

MAY 14. Fine morning, with the clouds high, and a roistering wind from the southwest. Strawberries are in bloom. We put in sweet corn yesterday, and melons.

I shot a woodchuck that has been marauding in our garden.

Two excursions to the hills in the last few days, one to Pelham, one to Belchertown. The woods are full of beauty, the first glories of spring. We are rich, in this valley, in wild flowering shrubs. The shadbush is the commonest, a white mist upon the hillsides, even among the pines. The spicebush, with its gleam of gold, is now passing, but the lovely and fragrant sassafras, especially on southern slopes in the woods, is just at its best. In old fields, along the worn ground of brook bottoms, I saw the ruddy glow of the high-bush huckleberries, and in the hedges and fences the chokecherries, with their neatly rounded blossoms, are coming on. I looked for the shy hobblebush, the finest treasure of the spring woods, but found none at all in blossom, and the dogwood and azaleas are riches yet to come.

The insolence of those who would make over a world which they have never taken the pains to look at, much less to understand! Man will succeed with nature, not by opposition, but as he works with it, as I with my bees. To understand is the first requisite. As for my neighbors, "I never meddle with saying what a man should doe in the world; there are overmany others that doe it; but what myself doe in the world." This I found the other day in Montaigne.

MAY 15. I started a glass observation hive in my study window. It has room for only one brood frame with glass on both sides, so that I can watch every movement of the bees. I brought in a frame from one of the colonies with worker and drone brood, considerable honey and pollen, but no queen or queen cells. I have bored a hole through the window frame so that they can have easy access to the open air. What I want to study especially this year is the building of queen cells, and the raising, in a colony without a queen, of a new queen. I plan to make careful daily notes.

In the hills the dogwood is just beginning to bloom. I am hard at work.

I have moments, in these days of national gloom, financial depression, "hard times," when I feel it my duty to be sad, or at least cynical—but cannot be—not in spring. I am like that chap in Boswell's life of Samuel Johnson, mourning the fact that he could not be a philosopher, because "cheerfulness was always breaking through." So much is wrong, but not my hills.

MAY 17. Today I traveled to our nearest city, and as I stood there in the moving street, my heart went out with new warmth to all the people going by. All kinds, poor, rich, ugly, beautiful, sad, sick, sunburned, happy, robust, cheap, silly, old, young, lame. Nevertheless, I thought, they are the best we have in this world. They are *all* we have: everything goes back to these strange, moving people; everything comes out of them; we must, after all, make up our world of them. We must fashion our government out of them. Revolt as we may, there is no other or better material. And when all is said, how extraordinarily interesting they are! What possibilities are tied up within them. Every last soul of them, I thought, has a story in him—maybe even a poem. No, one cannot throw humanity overboard without throwing himself overboard. And if one would escape, he merely changes one group for another: nothing is different or better.

MAY 18. I am delighted with my new glass hive. I can get my nose down to within an inch or two of the bees, and with my magnifying glass and a strong light watch them as I never did before. I spent all of last evening at it. I want to know every process in the life of the bee. It is the time of the early honey flow, and my colonies in the orchard, to which I have just added extracting supers, do not belong to the unemployed. Everything depends upon building up strong colonies for the clover season, next month.

If a man would be purged of his egotism and come all sweet and humble, let him read that poem which is the thirty-eighth chapter of the Book of Job, let him nevermore make assertions, but be willing to ask, see, think, and be quiet. This is the poem for the scientist.

MAY 19. I spent last evening again watching the bees in my glass hive finish the first queen cell and start another. They are beginning now to be active during the day, bringing in nectar and pollen. I have already seen several curious and amusing things that, in all my twenty years of beekeeping, I never saw before.

Everything is in anything: be still, then, sit where you are: beauty and wisdom are here. Serenity is not intellectual: it is centered emotion.

Man, as contrasted with the bees, has unsharable experiences. The bee has none. It is by these unsharable experiences that man has progressed.

I read of Franz Daniel Pastorius, who led the Germans to Pennsylvania in 1683, that "he was a lover of gardens and of bees." So many good, quiet men have loved bees.

I know no more of God than my honeybees of me, and yet I know—

If I cannot grasp God myself, I can look at some of His works, touch thus the hem of His garment.

MAY 20. This day positively hot and sultry. Hard at my desk in the forenoon. First orioles and goldfinches seen today. Also the bobolinks are here. There is no depression on this hillside!

I saw *Hamlet* played this evening by amateurs. I have seen *Hamlet* in my lifetime I think some fifteen or twenty times, played by several of the greatest players known to our stage, and some, certainly, of the worst. It is one play that no actors can wholly spoil.

As I grow older I enjoy *Hamlet* less and *The Tempest* more. Hamlet is too young: too full of the fevers, the doubts, the extremes of youth. He has not yet decided whether it is better to be or not to be. One tires of him.

But Prospero knows that life is good: he is wise with experience and with thought. He has stilled his beating mind, conquered his Caliban, and set free his Ariel. He has come to love his fellow men: "Please you, draw near." Turning now to Shakespeare, I turn oftenest to *The Tempest*.

MAY 22. Behold in me a miserable sinner. When I should be hard at work in my study I walk out into my garden to watch the young bees playing in front of their hives, and the catbirds singing like angels in the apple trees —and stealing the bees—and the tall tulips all in bloom, and the new corn pushing up through the brown earth, and the grassland I sowed a fortnight ago now coming green with clover and redtop and herd's-grass. It is

deliciously sunny and warm this morning—
and all still and sweet—to those who follow
the paths of iniquity.

After having considered all the problems of
the earth—with such absurd seriousness, such
comic importance!—I may, next year, or the
year after that, stop a moment and be happy.
As if peace conferences ever made peace! Or
wars made friendly nations! Or money won
joy! Or fame satisfied the spirit of man! So
absurd, so serious, so irresistibly comic! Next
year, then, or the year after that, I shall stop
and be happy.

MAY 26. This is a memorable day for the bee
people. I saw the first blossoms of the white
clover, but the honey flow from that source—
the best we have—will not begin for a week
or ten days. (It did not really begin for a
month—June 27th.)

The first new queen was born today in my
glass hive. Two queen cells remain unopened
—and will probably now be destroyed. I spent
a long time this evening, with my magnifying
glass and a strong light, watching the little
new virgin and her worshipful subjects.

This is the month of the year when "longen folk to gon on pilgrimages." I too! To walk straight away from work and home, to the hills and the open country roads, and new thoughts—

> *"With a new-coined day to fling away,*
> *And all the stars to spend."*

"Let 'im work at it," says Knox of the Hill Farm, when he sees a man trying to do a fool thing. "Let 'im work at it," says he cheerfully, knowing well that he will soon work himself out of it, or through it. Or, if it happens by long chance not to be a fool thing, why it is work that will prove it and establish it. "Let 'im work at it." Is there a better motto, more tolerant, wiser?

"Do I contradict myself? Well, then, I contradict myself." Do I make rash statements—mistakes? Well, then, I make rash statements and mistakes.

MAY 29. My glass hive grows more fascinating. On Saturday the 27th the workers, assisted by the jealous young queen, pulled down one of the two remaining queen cells

by gnawing through it at the rear and yesterday, the 28th, the queen herself aiding with
ferocity, destroyed the second, and killed the
feeble occupant, which leaves her, still a virgin, in lonely majesty. She marches proudly
across the comb, attended by her courtiers. It
seems a cruel business, but Queen Elizabeth
beheaded Mary Queen of Scots—and a good
job, too.

I am absorbed every moment of these gorgeous spring days: at my desk in the mornings, in the garden or fields in the afternoons.

SUNDAY. I spent a considerable part of this
sleepy Sunday afternoon trying to get a really
good look at a pair of Maryland yellow-
throats which have recently arrived in our
neighborhood and seem likely to take up lodg-
ings near us. They are easy to hear, often hard
to see. Their often-repeated cry, "chu-weechy,
chu-weechy, chu-weechy," is so loud and
plain that it suggests a much larger bird than
this warbler really is. One can see the very
tree or bush from whence the sound comes
and never get a good look at the bird itself.
I heard one calling to me this afternoon as
plainly as could be:

"I beseech you, I beseech you."

Not being able to resist such a plaint, I ran for my field glasses and followed cautiously down the hill. No sooner had I come near the hiding place than all was still, and presently from a more distant spot in the tangle I again heard the call:

"I beseech you, beseech you."

So I followed again, fairly creeping along. A flash of wings, a gleam of color and I was again disappointed. So I sat there on the hillside and waited. So many times in my life I have had things I desired not by seeking but by waiting. Presently I heard the shy singer again in a kind of wild mockery; not "I beseech you," but "witchery, witchery, witchery."

"Witchery it is," I said aloud and turned homeward.

But later, as if regretful of such coyness toward a friend, I came abruptly upon the shy singer herself. She was sitting quite fearlessly in a clump of forsythia, a delightful and beautiful little charmer.

It is pleasant enough to have these warblers here again, though later in the season their unchanging note grows strident and hard,

lacking the variety and interest of such birds
as the song sparrow.

If one feels lonely, how reassuring the
thought of friends never yet met.

Today on the hill road toward Belchertown I came across an old farmhouse in an
old field with stone walls all about it and a
great elm above it, and lilacs at the doorway.
I stopped for a long time to look at it. In some
other time, some other life than this, I shall
choose me just such a small place as this, a
small quiet place. There will be trees in it,
and little fields, and hills not far away, and
bees and honeysuckles and lilacs in the door-
yard—and I shall have One Book to write all
my life long and no one shall know anything
about it, or about me—I shall not try to do
anything Great, or Important, but only what
I love most.

MAY 31. We put in a third planting of sweet
corn, for a succession: the other plantings are
well up. We applied the calyx spray to the
apple trees. The irises are now blooming profusely in the new bed we set out a year ago:

Lent Williamson especially fine, also the dependable Pallada.

Much rain has turned all the meadows into green. I think of Walt Whitman's description of the grass:

"The handkerchief of the Lord,
   A scented gift and remembrancer, designedly dropt,
   Bearing the owner's name someway in the corners."

I seem to be doing nothing of any account these days—except to enjoy.

I had great pleasure today reading a list of old bee books, in which for several years I have been much interested, just received from Colonel W—— of Devon, England. It contains the most interesting notes. I wish I could walk down into Devon, such a morning as this, where I tramped with a pack on my back so many years ago. I remember the low hills of Devon and at evening the odor of burning peat moss—and the plovers whistling. How I should like to talk with this man about his bees at Westholm Maines, ten miles from Exeter. I should find him, I think, a kindred spirit!

JUNE

IN THE COUNTRYMAN'S YEAR

"Farming is a very fine thing, because you get such an unmistakable answer as to whether you are making a fool of yourself, or hitting the mark."—GOETHE.

CHAPTER III

JUNE IN THE COUNTRYMAN'S YEAR

JUNE 2. A wonderful warm June day: the first real day of summer. Everything lush and green. I never saw my meadow more luxuriant. I manured it heavily this spring, and there have been copious rains. The blackberries are coming into bloom, but not yet the raspberries. I put extra supers on several of my beehives.

An old colored woman, overworked, not well, most of her generation dead and gone, her one son ungrateful, her husband a burden, I heard today *singing.*

I believe most in the America that does not get into the newspapers.

I have been thinking today of writing a letter of advice to the President of China. I would not for a moment think of advising the President of the United States, but I know so little about the Chinese that I can easily tell them what they ought to do.

JUNE 5. A still, close, hazy, intimate day—one I love. Never have I known the fruit trees so heavily set, not only apples but peaches, pears, plums and quinces. Even my English walnut tree, a shy bearer so far, though now a dozen years old, has quite a crop in prospect, if the squirrels leave us any of it. There are also good crops of strawberries, raspberries and blackberries in sight, not yet ripe, of course. A promise of a good year.

Once I thought the only bird in this locality that fed on honeybees was our saucy and pugnacious kingbird. I discovered, long ago, my mistake. I am extremely fond of catbirds, but when food is scarce and they are feeding a young family they will dart down in front of the hives and snatch the bees: and today I discovered the cinnamon-brown female oriole —the Baltimore oriole—sitting on one of the hives. As I watched her she hopped down on the entrance board from time to time, snapped up a heavily loaded and therefore slow-moving bee and flew back to the hive top, where she bit her prey in two, eating the head and rejecting the abdomen. It must have been a lightninglike process, since there was no evidence that the bees tried to sting her. By the remnants of her feast, which I examined afterwards, she must have destroyed over a hundred bees in the space of a few minutes. However destructive the kingbird, at least he is a sportsman and takes his prey in the air, while in full flight.

We have in an adjoining town an old book-binder, a skillful mender of manuscripts, whom I like to visit. He has marvelously long delicate fingers: his nearsighted but adequate eyes are fitted to the microscope he often works with. He loves beautiful, perfect work, the kind of work that is slow to do, that is finished reluctantly; and the world has always hurried him, bullied him, underpaid him, as it does all artists. People do not see that he is putting his soul into these scraps of paper, these drops of pulp and paste: they do not appreciate the skill with which he handles his pen.

"This," he said helplessly to me, the last time I went to see him, "is the kind of a man I am."

"I know," I said, "and they will not let you be that kind of a man: they insist upon your being something else."

"That's it, that's it," he said eagerly. "They will not judge me according to my capacity."

Coming home after my last visit to the old manuscript mender, I chanced upon an observation by Professor Santayana, in a book I picked up quite by accident, which seemed a kind of generalization upon the experience:

"To be poor in order to be simple," says Santayana, "to produce less in order that the product may be more choice and beautiful, and may leave us less burdened with unnecessary duties and useless possessions—that is an ideal not articulate in the American mind."

JUNE 6. Hot. White clover now blooming profusely. Since the passage of the apple blossoms the bees have had a rather bare cupboard. My work goes too slowly. I have a vagrant, enjoying mind—which is contrary to all the sober rules. I should be digging into the *War Period of American Finance*. What, with the wood thrush singing? I should be turning over Willis' *Federal Reserve System*. What, with June just outside my window, and the new growth coming on the hemlock trees, and the warm sharp scent of the blackberry blossoms?

What we *select* is ours: this of riches, friends, learning, beauty. Personality is selection: to accept everything is to be nobody.

I suspect there are higher purposes in writing than our own enlargement, our own release, our own comfort—but a writer of necessity writes what he *is* and what he *must*. Let it go at that! Even some men on fire with a passion for objective truth, I suspect, write to release thoughts that might otherwise burst them. The scientist expresses his mind as the poet his creative passion: but it is a mark of all great writing, of whatsoever kind, that it somehow releases the soul of man: the poor caged spirit seeking in the beauty of the world, or in the lives of the brave and noble of the past, some balm for the brevity of life, some friend for the loneliness of it, some strength for the weakness of it. The little soul that we are, carrying about a corpse (as Marcus Aurelius says), yet singing a little each day, yet enjoying the hills and the trees—forgetting for a moment the past—ceasing for a moment to think of the future—is there not something beautiful about that?

I also am a Besotted Reader, often lost, as I was last night, in a book. In a world that sometimes seems evil and hard, I consort at will with strange and brave and noble men and women. When I read history I am conscious of the aristocracy of my forebears: my marvelous heritage. I come of an ancient and notable family: I am of the Human Race.

JUNE 7. In Pelham woods today I found the pink azalea blooming, filling all the air with spicy fragrance. On little knolls, or where the woods were deep, it lighted up the landscape

like a flame. It comes before the hardy laurel
ventures out, while the wild apples yet retain
their bloom. By old stone walls the blackberry brier spreads a mist of white, and once
I saw a locust tree that hummed with many
bees.

If we but knew it, we are already immortal.

I heard the other day someone telling of
Dr Peabody, of the Harvard Medical School,
how at the last, when he knew his life was
measured, when he was suffering constant
pain from an incurable disease, he went on
working, studying, teaching—and his face
began to glow and he appeared a happy man,
though to the friends who saw him being cut
down in his prime, his great work unfinished,
it all seemed stark tragedy. But he lived his
few remaining moments joyfully. He did not
bemoan his past or fear his future. He had no
silly idea that he was indispensable, that there
were not other men, in the millions of years
yet to come, who could finish what he had begun. He was doing well all he could do: he
was using his tools—that is, himself—as long
as he could, and as well as he could, to the

end. What more? What more? Any man who can do that will pass with a shining face.

JUNE 12. Cloudy and warm. We are now having too much moisture and sunless weather. Reading in bed last night the waspish, dogmatic, egotistical, pessimistic and yet often wise, clear, witty and penetrating essays of Schopenhauer. In one of his chief principles, "Happiness depends much more on what is within than without us," he is, surely, correct.

"It is always the case that if a man affects anything, whatever it may be, it is just there that he is deficient."

How happily I crop acres that are not mine. Walking today I found my bees gathering nectar unhindered in the wide meadows and fields of my neighbors F—— and S——, where there are worlds of white clover blossoms. Sweet brigandry! Wherever thoughts bloom I take them. What are names or titles to me? But I visit only those flowers that yield me nectar—mine by right of what I am.

How eagerly we seek out men who are only partly alive, but who see or hear more keenly, think more clearly—enjoy life more intensely!—than we do: and try thus to shine a little with borrowed effulgence.

Think what it would mean to find a man who was *all* alive: incandescent, glowing, shining. Think what a torch in the black and lonely night! Think how we should run from far and near to that man—that he might warm us in a cold world and light us through a dark one! Yet, if we found him, being such as we are, we should probably, straightway, destroy him. We should expect to find in him some material carbon, some literal combustible, that we could take in our hands and carry away, each to our own little hearthstone, to hover over it jealously and alone. We should never understand that it was fire from heaven, or we should deny, in the way of us as we are now, that it was real fire at all, and in the envy that is enraged by virtues we do not possess, we should douse it with the wet blankets of criticism and suspicion—even crucify it—until all the world was as dark again, as lonely and as dead, as our own souls.

JUNE 14. We cultivated our corn and potatoes and finished the fourth spraying of the apple trees, at the same time giving the potatoes a good treatment of pyrox.

Steve the Pole has just bought a horse and came around Tuesday to show him to me. A shaggy animal that fell sick the second day, I firmly believe, because of his astonishment at having a really good feed of oats. Steve got an old moth-eaten buggy at an auction and drove over here in triumph. His face was illuminated with satisfaction. He lives in a bare house, far from clean, his wife crawls with him all summer down the long rows of the onion fields while several scandalously healthy children squawl and sleep on the grassy margins. They all work prodigiously. I could make out a pathetic story of the lives of these people whom I know well: the ignorance, the language limitation, the exploitation, the want of standards of living that we regard as indispensable—yet, taken alone, it would be an absolutely false account of them. They are mainly a robust, healthy, happy people, working hard, full of hope, getting ahead. They quarrel more or less among themselves: some are tricky, some drink too much, and judged by our standards some are rough with their women and children—all that!—but upon the whole they are a vigorous, progressive stock which will one day form the human bedrock of these valleys.

So many writers fail in the primary requirement—of being great men. Their books give them away.

In any argument, if two men disagree, one is certain to be wrong; but if they agree, both are probably wrong.

JUNE 18. I was up at sunrise and went out into the dewy world—long shadows on the grass, the sun just touching the treetops, as fine a June morning as ever I saw in my life. I took with me a box and picked it full of strawberries from the garden bed, only the ripest and sweetest I could find. There was a faint scent from somewhere up the hill—mock oranges, I think—and I could see, not far away, the heavy pink peonies of the flower garden in heavy bloom. It was still, still, scarcely a bird note—for the early-morning concert was past—but far off across the valley I could hear the rumble of a farm wagon.

—When my box was heaping full of as fine fruit as was ever known to king or kaiser— probably finer—I came into the quiet house. I set out a tall bottle of milk, and good new bread and butter, and a cake of my own honey (last year's, for the new honey is not yet capped).

"I'll be as reckless as ever I please," I said, and having dusted the berries with sugar— not too much—I poured over them the best of the cream. So then I sat on the open porch where I could look across the awakening hills, and had a breakfast that the gods might envy.

(When my director and mentor is away I feel too big and clumsy for the kitchen. The dishes overwhelm me. I tip them over. Things get wet, and I can find nothing to wipe them on. The towels degenerate mysteriously into soggy wads. The coffeepot loses itself under the sink, the butter melts down, the bacon burns.)

I rode today sixty-three miles in a motorcar to see this "wonderful New England country" —and saw little or nothing of it. No sooner had my thoughts alighted upon this hill, that sleeping valley, an entrancing bit of stream, or a roadside fernery, than I was snatched away to something else. I came home with nothing but a blurred sense of motion, wind in my face, and the countryside spinning dizzily by. I had far more the other day in a three-mile walk from here to Mill Valley. "Slowness," as Rodin said, "is beauty."

One test of happiness—or ecstasy, or contentment—is the absolute disappearance of the time sense. In complete absorption in labor or in contemplation we are unaware whether our moments are hours or days. We are immortal—strange paradox—for a moment!

To sit down of a morning at my desk and suddenly start upward to find it noon—and the call to come to luncheon—is not that perfect? I may consider afterwards that the product of my engrossing occupation is far from perfection, or that I have not produced as much as I hoped, but no one can rob me of the sense of fulfillment which comes of such complete absorption. I often have much the same experience when working in my garden or with my bees, wherein I live completely and intensely in the task, in the thought, in the beauty, of the moment. I dismiss the past; and the future has no terrors for me, since I never try to live in it until it arrives.

There are, however, serious disadvantages connected with this seemingly simple method. This morning, despatched hurriedly to town because the household cupboard was empty, I continued so absorbed that I walked straight past Harvey's market and did not bring up until I had reached the Baptist church. I stopped, laughing, and said to myself:

"That is the trouble with folks like me. We walk past the markets we intend to visit. And when we wind up in front of a church it is Monday and we can't get in—even if we wanted to."

I thought, also, that we sometimes walk, absently, full of our own joy, past many an old duty, many a monied opportunity, sometimes, unintentionally, past a good friend or a smiling child—penalties, surely, of the method. But . . .

JUNE. SUNDAY. Can there be, at one time, such contradictory emotions as a passion for quietude? This morning, early, walking down through the still garden with the slant sun upon the dewy grass and all about the sweet stillness of a perfect Sunday morning in summer, I felt such an emotion as I can call only a passion for quietude. I felt like treading softly, holding my breath, lest I break the crystal globe of stillness, or rend the gossamer web of silence.

In these recent days, working early and hard with brain and hand, not to excess in either, but with the complete joy of doing what one is completely absorbed in doing, studying and writing in the long mornings, working in the garden or orchard, or caring for the bees, in the afternoons, and then sometimes at evening, on hot dry days, going for a plunge in the cool water of the river—what could be more perfect?

I was recalling today the two mottoes of my father, who was a cavalry officer in the Civil War:

"When in doubt, charge!"

"Admit nothing to be a hardship."

Closely analyzed, one might ask if either was truly wise? Or either true? And yet they have, curiously, poignantly, the essential personality of my father in them. He lived by them: through them he communicated to his small world a sense of native power, an incentive to bold endeavor. He charged, indeed, too often when he doubted: he suffered unnecessary hardships which, if admitted, might have been avoided—but there he stood, clearcut, a bold, original, enduring spirit.

JUNE 20.   The click of the mower is heard in the land. Steve has begun the hay cutting at the lower end of our meadow. The crop where I put on manure this spring is tremendous, heavy alfalfa, as high as my waist. The strawberries are nearly gone, but the black cherries are coming in. I planted the last sweet corn today.

I have been listening to the bobolinks in Farley's meadow, whose song "runs down, a brook of laughter, through the air."

Strange, the real life of us, how detached, intimate, a world of its own, which, in revolving about the sun of its destiny, turns over also on its own axis. To see me going drably about my business is not to see me at all—the flame I keep burning within. It is the same, strangely, with you. Like stars in vast space, each in its own orbit, we are millions of light-years apart. We look at each other through dim telescopes, weigh each other in confused logarithms, test each other in cold spectra—and I burning hot with my own heat, and you with yours.

It is true enough, and sad enough, as Emerson says (in his essay on Goethe) that "we seldom see anybody who is not uneasy or afraid to live."

JUNE 21. Now the heavy sweet odor of the blackberries in my garden, cloying the summer air—too heavy sweet! And at dawn the full-toned catbird singing at my window. In the meadow the alfalfa is blooming in royal purple, a wide and generous pasture for the bees.

The days are hot and dry, and I rise at dawn to work, safe from interruption, at my desk on the open porch. Whenever I look up, there before me is spread the glory of the earth, distant hills across green meadows, and nearer at hand the busy doings of my garden and orchard. I can see the robins stealing the half-ripe cherries and I a laggard, letting them steal, thankful if at length we get enough for two pies.

This morning, in the midst of a sentence, I heard the roar of bees swarming, and a moment later the air above the hives was dark with them. I ran down with my veil and smoker and hive tools, and found them, presently, lighted in the top of a tall pear tree which I had to reach from a ladder set perilously against the uncertain branches and held below by the tremulous Steve. Sometimes they choose even more distressful places where they have to be shaken first into a large pail or boiler, covered with a rug and rushed to the new hive. But this morning I was able to cut the branch of the pear tree on which they hung and, by using caution, bring down the entire mass, weighing ten or a dozen pounds—some thirty thousand bees—and carry them across the orchard to the hive I had prepared to receive them.

I had spread down a white cloth in front of the opening, and when I gave the severed branch a vigorous shake, the entire mass of bees fell on the cloth and spread out immediately like spilled molasses. Some took at once to the air, others rushed hither and thither across the white cloth, wildly looking for their queen. I went down on my knees and likewise searched for Her Majesty, knowing that she would determine the action of the entire swarm. I have never yet clearly understood how or when a swarm of bees decides to go into a new hive, but nine times in ten they make their decision within a few minutes. At first they seem utterly confused. There is a strident, excited, restless note in the humming: but presently some of the workers near the hive entrance begin going in. Shortly the tone quiets down to a low, steady, contented hum—the voice of a satisfied community— and the entire mass, even four or five feet away, face about and begin to flow, a dark active stream, into the new hive. I kneel there watching the queen, knowing that if she goes in all is well: if she does not go in, and takes to the air, as sometimes happens, the work is all to be done over again.

I thought today as I was cutting down the swarm from the pear tree that if I were one of that highly developed colony, I should, if there were a free choice, be of the company of the scouts, off in the free air, looking for a

new and better world to live in. I do not easily
stay with the swarm.

Strange people going by—strange, miraculous!—deep in their own thoughts, their own
longings, their own sadness or joy, and I with
so little time to know them.

Why are they here? How did they come to
be what they are? Have they wisdom I do not
know, or folly I could physic? We might love
each other. Maybe one of them is almost perfect!

I have comfort, sometimes, these days,
thinking how the Emperor Marcus Aurelius,
having a true philosophy to guide his life,
kept on fighting the Quadi—until he died. A
philosophy is not to be retired into: no ship
that is not moving can be steered: but it is the
sursum corda of the man who is fighting the
Quadi of the far wilderness (or writing large
long, dull books!).

Did Marcus Aurelius conquer the Quadi?
I wonder. I don't know. Does anybody? If
the Quadi had conquered Marcus Aurelius,
would it have made any difference? Would
he not have known, equally well, how to live?

JULY

IN THE COUNTRYMAN'S YEAR

"Pleased with each food that Heaven to
  man supplies;
Yet oft a sigh prevails, and sorrows fall,
To see the hoard of human bliss so small."
—OLIVER GOLDSMITH, in *The Traveller.*

CHAPTER IV

JULY IN THE COUNTRYMAN'S YEAR

JULY. SUNDAY. What still sunny days we have now. And I alone in them, to be quiet. I have lived here upon this hillside for many years, and it seems to me I love it better with every changing season. I am up at dawn to be at my work—teasing along a wayward, tardy book

—but cannot keep long from my garden. Each hour or so I am out to see what new progress the tall hollyhocks that grow by the wall have made, or to pick and eat a handful of late strawberries, or to watch the bee people in front of the hives knitting their swift web of flight.

Yesterday we were haying in the meadow. A fine, great crop, half alfalfa, and heavy. I cannot bear the labor of earlier years but helped pitch on until I dripped with perspiration. I like to watch the great loads going in at the dark and gaping doorway of the barn: the smell of cattle there: the man on the load with his barbed hayfork, the pulley squeaking to the hoist rope—I like it all.

Today with several sharp passes of my hive tool I destroyed hundreds of drone cells in one of my bee colonies, each of which would have produced a bee that might have become the progenitor of vast families of bees. And this spring we gathered up several bushels—millions—of seeds from under our maple trees, every one of which might have made a new tree fifty feet tall, to live for a century or more, and itself produce countless billions of seeds. Yet not one of the seeds we gathered will ever grow; they decay on my compost heap. It is a wearying thought—the vast fecundity of nature, wherein birth is an infinitesimal chance: wherein growth after birth is only a remote possibility: wherein final maturity is not short of a miracle. How fortunate, then, to be here at all. To be alive on such a day in summer—and the wood thrush singing!

Some time ago I started to write a book on Democracy, but was constantly interrupted in the most ridiculous way by reality. No sooner had I set down a beautiful observation or generalization than one of my neighbors, especially H—— and W——, would come walking into the scene and, in spite of all I could do, insist upon being undemocratic. (And this, too, in an old New England town, which I heard a learned historian the other day call "the heart of American democracy.") Now what, I ask you, was an earnest writer to do under such circumstances? Was it better to stop my book, or to stop H—— and W——? After thinking it over I decided not to write a book on Democracy.

JULY 6. The lindens are in bloom—too sweet, but full of bees. First scattering ripe red raspberries. The field grasses were never better: the fescue in my meadow is as tall as my shoulder, and thick. The field corn is late: it has not observed the ancient New England rule: "knee-high for the Fourth of July."

Today, when I had an unexpected whiff of the wild grape blossoms, I said to myself:

"Of all odors, this is, surely, the sweetest."

As the season advances some one odor seems the best of all. Early in May it was the bloom of the flowering crab, then the apple blossoms, then the old-stock lilacs, and now the grape vies with the wild roses which, in the wasteland scarcely a stone's throw from my boundary, fill all the air with ravishing odors.

On such days I have this to regret, that my sense of smell is not what it was in earlier years. Wanted, someone to invent a pair of glasses for the nose. Why not? By one of the simplest of devices sight has been restored to age, the vision of youth recovered. Why not, now, the sense of smell?

In my earlier years I had an unusually keen sense of smell, inherited, I think, from my

father, who was a genius in this respect, but
the onset of the years has served to dim a
source of uncommon joy. Many of the most
exquisite and delicate odors that I remember
well in the past now escape me wholly, but
such a rank and stinging scent as that of the
blackberry brier, hot and sweet—like large-
lettered type to the eyes—gives me still the
old-time pleasure. And yesterday at the fruit
store the Italian handed me a melon to test,
and I had an unexpected delight at the odor
of it: but such joys, I regret, grow rarer with
the years. I can see nothing for it but to demand an invention of a kind of smellacles for
the nose.

I am somewhat comforted in my affliction,
however, by the discovery that the naturalist,
W. H. Hudson—one of the best of my recent
book friends—comments (in *Far Away and
Long Ago*) on his own loss of smell in his
later years, and considers it the common fate
of increasing age. Yet how vividly he recalls
the odors as well as the sights and sounds of
his youth there on the pampas. As a matter
of fact, no really deep sensual impression is
ever quite lost; and I think sometimes that
these stored-away and much-cherished odors

and sights and sounds increase in their enchantment as the rivalry of newer impressions begins to fade. How bright the woven tapestry of scenes long past but dear still to the memory: how sweet the odors of our youth.

But I would have a pair of smellacles if I could get them!

So brief—our best!

I read today in a famous literary supplement, a publication I usually prize, a review of a religious book that irritated me extremely. It was based upon the old argument that a mistaken idea must be retained because it is comforting. Because of "perplexities, sorrows and sins," there must somehow be ignorance to soothe them. Men are weak and sinful, and therefore require lies. Anything but to face life and be honest and clear! Thoughts hurt, therefore don't think: life is hard, therefore mystify it, drug it, dull it—everything but live it! Better, I think, a crust of real life than a banquet of beliefs that dull the soul.

JULY 10. Perfect summer weather. I have been talking with Cobb, a good friend and neighbor of mine. He has an interesting hobby—making studies of the song of the meadow lark. In the course of seven years he has recorded no fewer than 572 songs. While there are only slight variations in pitch, and the songs are only four to six notes in length, the variety is extraordinary. Each song is usually repeated five or ten times, often twenty.

I supposed, of course, that Cobb went to the fields to find his larks, but he told me that most of his records were made *in bed* in the wakeful early morning when, through the open window, he could hear the larks at their matins. I have a vision of him sitting there, propped up, with his pitch pipe at his lips and his notebook on his knee, setting down his records. One song he recalls vividly, repeated eight times and never heard again—the Meistersinger of all the larks! The effect was the repose that nature suggests but rarely satisfies. Cobb says he listens not to record, but records in order to listen, which is the test of one who really goes to nature to enjoy.

JULY 12. I am not working well these days, but I am working—taking what I can, living as much as I can, and not anxious. If I cannot master the great things, I can enjoy the small. I have been thinning the fruit on my apple trees, since there is a heavy oversetting. Two of the finest of my Baldwins show signs of splitting with their burden, and I am having Whitcomb, the blacksmith, make me iron rods to hold them together. Thank God for the precious small things of the earth, and days like these when the hills are a benediction, and the shorn meadows, peace.

Give me long books, read a little at a time, picked up in stolen moments, or comfortably taken to bed. How one lives into them! Pepys' *Diary,* Carlyle's *French Revolution,* Thoreau's *Journal!* Boswell, which I have been re-reading, is assuredly one of the best; few books I know in which one can enter more fully into the life and mind of a complete human being, or better enjoy the wit of choice spirits. "No, Sir," says Johnson, commenting on the proper method of diverting one's distressing thoughts. "No, Sir. To attempt to *think them down* is madness. He should have a lamp constantly burning in his bedchamber during the night, and if wakefully disturbed, take a book, and read, and compose himself to rest." This recipe have I often tried and know well that it works.

It is nothing to me that some of Johnson's dicta have proved erroneous. I like men with stout opinions! "Nothing odd," said he, "will do long," which is probably true, but the instance he gave was unfortunate. *"Tristram Shandy,"* he argued, "did not last." But today ten, possibly a hundred, men read *Tristram Shandy* to one who ever heard of his own *Rasselas,* or have read *The Rambler.*

Speaking of *Rasselas,* I remember well my own first acquaintance with Dr Johnson. In my father's library, in which every volume contained a bookplate with the dire warning: "The ungodly borroweth and payeth not again," there was a book in which *Paul and Virginia* and *Rasselas* were bound up together—strange company! I remember with what breathless interest I read the first, and with what expectation, lured onward, I began *Rasselas.* To this day I recall—for I could not finish it and never afterwards tried to read it —the sensation of being lost in sonorous mountains. It is no boy's book! And yet I felt that there was something in it that was strong and noble. If I did not understand what it was, I did not wholly forget it—and that is something to be said of any book.

Boswell's book is one of those I call robust, healthy, sound—a good antidote for the sickliness of the age: the record of a great spirit struggling with the flesh.

I have thought of a good epitaph for my tombstone:

"He who led an interrupted life lies here at last uninterrupted."

JULY 13. Being weary today at my desk, so that the strength and the joy had gone out of me, I went into my garden, and there in the morning sunshine, among the apple trees, I began opening my hives to look for queen cells, to see what must be done to increase the storage of honey. For a time I was dull and slow, wholly intent upon the processes of my labor wherein much depends upon an exact knowledge of the law of the hive. Presently I was conscious of a bird singing in the apple tree just over my head. It was the "easy—so easy—so easy" of one of our most cheerful neighbors, the song sparrow.

"So easy indeed," said I. "It is precisely the advice I need—on a fine morning like this, in summer."

"So easy—so easy—so easy," responded my friend.

"Indeed so," said I. "So easy to be happy on a day like this. Such warm sunshine, such cool shadows I think I never knew before. Such odors: such sounds!"

"So easy—easy—easy," agreed the little bird.

It was then I began to think of the evils of the world, so long weighing heavily upon my spirit—wars, strikes, poverty, hunger, greed, cruelty. It may be, I thought, that men will have to be turned back to the soil for a thousand years or so to exorcise them. It may be that the remedy, as in ancient times, lies here upon the open land.

For I thought, as I knelt there by my hives, of the absolute veracity of these natural processes. Here one comes to know the immutable logic of cause and effect. One cannot fool a hive of bees! There is no gambling short cut to honey: no getting by with clever words. Reward rests exactly upon effort, effort exactly upon knowledge. Man is constantly forgetting this law, becoming impatient of this order, despising the slow processes of creation and growth, seeking by silly force, or sillier duplicity, to satisfy his greed by short cuts. We who kneel by our hives know well that it cannot be done. We know that the attempt to do it results in what we see abroad in the world today: hunger, poverty, unemployment, hatred, bitter depression and dismay. It cannot be done!

To the writer: Stop! Having said it—the quick, live thing you have in your mind—stop!

How strange! Men are so rarely surprised at evil, so easily at goodness.

I had a friend who stumbled along painfully with many doubts, but with an absorbed interest in life. One year he fell into a certainty, and that was the end of him.

JULY 14. I have traveled and tramped in Scotland, but never really had need to, since we have a bit of Scotland near at home. I mean the island of Nantucket, where of a summer day one may also find warm moors

and mists and the sea wind. I have come in recent years, during fugitive visits, to love well
this aromatic paradise—sweet fern and bay-
berry and tangles of wild red roses. One can
be lost there, and yet be happy; there are the
three simplicities: the sky, the sea, and the
moor. Dimness of soul—what could be worse?

JULY 15. This year, as never before since we
lived upon this hillside, we have the wood
thrushes with us. I think it is due to the woody
deeps near us to the south, and to our own
trees, grown large with the years. No bird I
know has such a wealth of mystery and wild
music in its hidden song—unless it is, occasionally, the vireo. The brown thrushes nest
in our garden, and we see them familiarly, a
beautiful and graceful bird with a fine song,
but the wood thrush, hiding in its coverts, a
sensitive spirit, rarely shows itself.

JULY 21. Now is the heyday of summer:
everything voluptuously in growth. It is the
full, warm, robust middle age of the year,
with good health and thriving normal life.
The earth, ripe with products as well as promise, smiles now with full contentment. The

corn in my field is even with my shoulder, the rowen alfalfa, freshly green, has come eagerly to the second blossoming. All the cut meadows, in spite of dry weather, are again greening; the potatoes, not yet blighted, carpet their broad acres, and the onions and tobacco, the chief commercial crops of our valley, are at their best. They will indeed grow larger, but will never again look so well. The early peaches in my orchard—the Mayflower—hang loaded with red-ripening fruit, never so abundant as this year. The raspberries are past, or nearly past, but the blackberries are coming on, though the fruit, maturing in dry weather, is of poorer quality than usual. The early apples—the Yellow Transparent—are full-grown, nearly ready to use, but the later apples, especially the Spies, are backward. All the hives are filling with honey: I shall soon be taking off some of the supers. In the garden we have zinnias and calendulas and hollyhocks at their best, and great red and white roses. Surely, a good, abundant, smiling time of the year!

Here I live. After wandering, this valley is my home, this very hillside: these green acres.

I want no other. This is my progress, the succession of the seasons; this my reward, the product of the earth. Here may I think and love and work. Here have I lived and here I would die, for of all places under the sun I know of none that contents me better.

Nothing is required of me, I think, that cannot be done with joy.

Stop here and be happy: where find a likelier place?

JULY 27. Rain in the night, all night long. It has been hot and dry, a week or more of burning sunshine, parched meadows and withering corn. The earth of fields and garden has grown powdery dry and at cultivation lifted a smoke of dust. The hills were hazy, and the leaves of the trees looked parched and sick. The ripening fruit has been coming pinched and seedy and sour.

But last night came the rain, all night long. I awakened in the dark with the cool sweet breath of it upon my face. I lay there, still and happy, and listened to the rain come down. There was not a breath of wind, not one gusty shower. It was as though nature had drawn a long sigh and, repenting her hot anger of past days, had begun to weep softly, copiously, to assuage the fever of the burning earth.

I heard the rain tapping on the roof, whispering among the leaves of the ash tree next my window, drumming in the downspouts. I could smell the fragrance—the unforgettable fragrance—of new rain upon parched verdure and thirsty dust. It came straight down and filled all the night with comfort and releasement.

How pleasantly, then, my thoughts went out to the suffering fields, sharing the gratitude of the grass, pausing at the edge of the corn to listen to the sibilant leaves cupped to the blessing of the sky. I stopped by the withering blackberry rows and thought of the blessed moisture soaking into that ashy soil, and the roots, deep hidden, reaching out like thirsty children to the welcome bosom of mother earth.

From time to time the downpour slackened, and then I heard the dripping among the trees and from the eaves of the house, exactly like hushed voices telling one another sleepily of their joy. I tried to catch what it was they were saying, but never a word could I make out, but knew that it was all in verse that they spoke in their sleep: the poetry of the rain. Presently I could hear a renewal of the rappings and tappings, as though the earth, still unsatisfied, was telegraphing the heavens for more—and then, presently, a new largess of the rain.

It seemed to me that all these days past I too have been withering with the dry earth, parched for want of the rain of heaven, and I too am eased and relieved: my thirst quenched in a new serenity. I slept again, but lightly, conscious all through the night of the voices of the rain.

At dawn I was up and out to see gray clouds hovering low in the sky. It seemed as if all nature, trees and grass and vines and flowers, was literally lifting up its head in praise of God. Some of the birds, deep hidden among the trees, were chirping their joy and some, especially the robins, were abroad upon the field and lawn, heads up and tails down, eagerly hopping about.

So I went down into it and was glad to feel the rain on my face and in my hair. I, too, like the wilting verdure, drew myself erect. I saw how greedily the curled leaves of the apple trees were holding this nectar of the gods, and each separate long needle of the red pines kept a pearllike drop at its point, so that the whole tree glistened with a kind of radiance; and the tall-grown asparagus had put on filmy necklaces of jewels to welcome the dawn. How good this day: how fine the rain: how happy am I. We that thirst have had our fill.

"Praised be our Lord for our sister Water, who is very serviceable unto us, and humble, and precious, and clean."

Talk of luxury! This day, after the rain, walking in my garden, I heard among my early cabbages strange flutterings, splashings, chirps of delight. What could it be? I tiptoed carefully along the rows until I surprised the nymph herself. One of the large green cabbage leaves had caught and held a veritable bowl of water during the rain, and here one of my favorite song sparrows was bathing. What dainty flutterings and splashings, what joyous chirping! After days of dry weather, how good this pool of cool water so conveniently provided by nature. After a moment of this gay sport my sparrow darted out of her bath, but an instant later was down in another green pool, and presently I saw her try a third. Talk of luxury!

JULY 28. The sweet corn is tasseling out: we have had our first new potatoes.

You may know the true gardener by his willingness to kneel in the earth—willing knees and a strong back. He loves the feel of the soil: he loves to step around in his garden paths in such warm moist mornings of July as this, when the vegetation can almost be seen to grow. He loves every row of corn, every hill of melons, every clump of tall holly-hocks: and because he loves he disciplines, prunes, thins.

I like all things in season: sour strawberries from Texas in March partly destroy our own luscious product of June and July. So much labor wasted in the telescoping of nature's program.

JULY 31. We add yearly to the teeming popu-lation of our hillside. To our 400,000 honey-bees and many other insects and birds, our predatory skunks and rabbits, the snake that lives in our garden wall and came out in May to cast its skin, we have added recently a swift lizard. I have seen him several times on a warm stone near the garden steps. When I come upon him he darts like a flash into a crevice.

But we have one fat woodchuck less than we had. Some time ago I saw in the corner of my prize alfalfa field a heap of yellow earth thrown up, and found there a yawning woodchuck hole. A day or so later I saw madame herself—or monsieur?—sitting on her pyramid and looking warily at her little world. She was a big one, well fattened on my alfalfa and the tender tops of my choicest peas. The robber! When she saw me she ducked her head, as well she might, and slid away into her hole.

We have a neighbor, old Mr F——, who is a graduate master of animal lore. He is versed in the habits of woodchucks, skunks, rabbits, weasels; he knows how to set traps, lay deadfalls, put up twitch nooses. He dares lift a skunk out of a box trap with his bare hands; he knows where and how to grasp a fox so that the sharp white teeth do not fasten upon him.

Old Mr F—— came down to look at my woodchuck. I did not summon him, nor expect to pay him. He heard somehow by grapevine telegraph that there was a chance in my meadow to exercise his magic.

"A fine old, big, fat one," said he. "Do you want me to catch 'im?"

"I do," said I, "and I'll lend a hand. I hear you're an expert."

"Waal," said he, "I don't know as to that; but when I kin see 'em, I kin catch 'em."

A little later he came down with a stubby broom and a good-sized wooden box. A crowd of eager boys followed after him as they must have followed the original Rip Van Winkle. I provided several galvanized iron tubs and pails and a barrel.

"I see," said I, "that you have faith. You've brought a box to put the woodchuck in."

"Sure," said he. "I ain't guessin'."

We all joined in the task of bringing water from the house until we had every pail, tub, and boiler filled, to say nothing of the barrel, and all placed in a circle around the woodchuck hole. Old Mr F—— was in his element; he stepped about like the colonel of a regiment. He was happy, he was important, he was dignified.

"Now," said old Mr F——, "we'll surprise the old lady."

With that we began swashing the water into the hole, the boys full of excitement, working as boys never worked before.

"Hold back now on that there bar'l," commanded our colonel. "We'll need her later."

We could hear the water gurgling down into the burrow. Half the boys were on their knees looking in, and the other half were on top of them, looking over their shoulders.

"I don't believe there's any woodchuck down there," shouted one young skeptic.

"You wait," responded the brave commander.

Suddenly we heard a gurgling sound, then a snort, and a great furry head emerged at the entrance of the hole. A moment later, not liking our company, she dodged back again.

Now was the moment of crisis: now was the time to charge!

"Hey there, lads!" cried the commander. "Git that bar'l! Hold 'er boys, hold 'er steady now. Douse her in!"

We poured in a new inundation.

"She'll come now, you bet," cried old F——. "You bet she'll come now."

A moment later there was a tremendous gurgling and splashing and up came the woodchuck looking for the moment as big as a Newfoundland dog. Before she could run or dodge back old F——, quick as a flash, had pinned her down with his stubby broom and then, reaching one bare arm down into the burrow, he caught her by the nape of the neck and held her up, squirming, and showing her sharp white teeth. Pop—she went into his wooden box. In a moment he had nailed down the slats.

"I knowed I'd get 'er," said old F—— triumphantly.

A moment later the entire army, officer and men, were marching up the road carrying the prize of war.

And so the population of our hillside is depleted by one fat woodchuck.

AUGUST

IN THE COUNTRYMAN'S YEAR

---

*"I will take a branch of gooseberries
from the old bush in the garden and go and
preach to the world."*

CHAPTER V

AUGUST IN THE COUNTRYMAN'S YEAR

AUGUST 1. It is the beginning of the golden-rod and, in the long warm evenings, the cricket. Now the blackberries are ripe, and the new green corn, most delicious of vege-tables, is plentiful. Bees hum in the ivy on the wall, and the early apples turn their red-

105

dened faces to the sun. Hollyhocks are blooming, tall and stately, by the wall, and we have full-blown zinnias for the breakfast table. Now there are moments of quiet I enjoy.

I read this in a chapter on Confucius—a proof of his wisdom:

"That whereby man differs from the lower animals is little. Most people throw it away."

I sat last night, in the heat of the evening, and watched the lights come out, one by one, upon the western hills—little pin points in the vast darkness—intimations of the light beyond. Pin points in the dark: so our knowledge; so little the seen compared with the unseen.

AUGUST 3. I have rarely known hotter days in New England. Parching winds from the South, all the earth dry and hot. At evening we went for a plunge off the rocks into the Connecticut River at Whitmore's.

For a long time I asked much and got little; now I ask little and get much.

I have been reading a fine book: Sabatier's life of St Francis of Assisi. It is said that among his followers there were some "whom it did not satisfy to be saints, but who also wished to appear such."

AUGUST 4. I have been taking off more of my new honey, most excellent in quality and in far larger quantity than last year. I shall really make some money out of the crop, besides having an abundant supply for the family.

Steve is harvesting onions on my lower acres. He was discouraged in hot July, for the struggle with the witch grass was unremitting. At one time he was ready—at least he said so—to plow up his crop: he now has the best field of onions in the neighborhood and smiles broadly every time I go down to see him.

A good fat time of the year.

"There is something," says Emerson, "not solid in the good that is done *for* us."

I am so much interested in life I have no time to worry about it.

A weak tree drops its apples before they are ripe: a weak writer his books.

There is something abhorrent, ghastly—something offensive to every instinct of comeliness, order, beauty—in this characteristic of machines, that they will not die. Their angular, rusty, immeasurably ugly skeletons mar our sunny fields, corrupt the shores of peaceful streams, lie ghastly by pleasant roadsides. A man dies, or an animal, or a tree, and the willing earth soon takes them to itself, grows a flower where they lie, works over them patterns in moss and lichens. But the dead machine does not die: there it lies inimical to life, to beauty, to order. Man seems unable to efface the ugliness he has made.

It is not so difficult for a man to be elected president, or governor, or mayor: and even make out to *be* president, or governor, or mayor. But no man ever yet has been, or ever will be, elected to the high place of artist, or poet, or saint, or prophet. The greatest, most desirable, most profitable of offices are within a man's own choice: he elects himself: opportunity is absolutely free.

AUGUST 12. The early peaches are all gone now; but the red plums are ripe. I have been taking off some of the finest comb honey from my hives that ever I saw. In the late afternoon I put a bee-escape just under the top super, and by the next day all the bees have left it and I can easily lift it off. Each super contains twenty-eight sections of about a pound each, most of them well filled and perfectly capped. The blackberries, which were more or less of a failure this year, are past, but the early apples are coming in, the Wealthy and the Gravenstein. We have had the first of our sweet corn—yellow bantam—most delicious. A cob of sweet corn ought to be pulled, husked, and put in the pot, like a brook trout, while it is still flapping. Even an hour's delay seems to destroy something of the perfect flavor: and at its best there is no vegetable known to man finer than a cob of yellow bantam corn—steamy from the kettle, with new butter and just a pinch of salt.

The goldenrod, sign and symbol of autumn, is yellowing brightly along all the roadsides, the pink of the hardhack in old sour fields is fading into dingy brown: it has had its season of beauty. I like the smell of the leaves of the walnut tree as I pass, and yesterday I stood long by the tall Hubam clover for the breath of its sweetness and the busy sound of bees among its blossoms. The tobacco cutting on the lower flats has begun: a plentiful crop; and the Poles are harvesting the early onions: the sets. Never, I think, has the earth given such an impression of teeming plenty.

Rest is as much a law of life as labor, but we forget it.

In time of suffering and trouble try coming to the country to be free and simple. Get your hands daily into the soil. It may not be your only work; you may wish also to teach Greek, or write novels, or make butter bowls, or work in a garage, but somewhere, somehow, each day get back to your own garden, or tree, or grass plot. It may be that you will come presently to serenity.

AUGUST 15. Yesterday I took up to the market a large basketful of my choicest honey, both in comb and in golden yellow bottles. I had expended no end of care in making everything perfect. I had polished off each section with two grades of sandpaper, removing every trace of propolis that adhered to the wood, so that it looked as white and fresh as the beautifully capped honey. Each comb was fitted into a little paper box with a cellophane window so that it could easily be examined: and upon each jar of the extracted honey I had pasted a label bearing my name and address.

But the moment I took my basket into the market I began to be curiously embarrassed. What a contrast between the seller and the buyer! How noble and independent the buyer: how disdainful! "I do not like this," says he, "show me something else. Is this a speck, a crack, a smudge, a nick, a knot?—take it away." Or he says, "I am sorry, Mr Smith. I will go across the street to Mr Jones."

How humble and courteous, in contrast, is the seller: how low-voiced, how diffident, how ingratiating! How passionate his desire to please!

I had felt mightily proud of my produce until I got well into the market, walking down the lane between boxes of well-laundered carrots and barbered beets and blushing tomatoes. I knew that my honey was as good as honey could be; but there was an accusing and intimidating look in the eye of the merchant so that I began at once to think of arguments to prove that I was in reality a fairly honorable man, bringing in a product that was reasonably good. But my long labor and care began to seem, after all, rather unimportant—even cheap.

It wasn't so much what was said, but a kind of terrific attitude of passivity and repletion. Who wanted any honey? People were already well filled with cauliflowers, canned beans, pickles, whole-wheat bread, factory pies—my glance swept swiftly around the crowded market—what room had they for the laborious product of my hives?

There was, in fact, in this market, and in the world, too much of everything, too many things to eat. Besides that, how wonderfully everything was painted up, dressed up, papered up! My eye caught a glimpse of packages of spaghetti with verses on them to incite the purchaser with a poetic rage to buy. Who wanted my unsung, unversed, unradioed, unadvertised honey? It was good honey, it was the best that those perfect artists and workers, the bees, could make, and I had added to it not a little labor of love, but there was some incitement, some final seductive charm, that was apparently wanting. I had no slogan—something like this perhaps: "Good honey for little money." There was no portrait, upon my box, of a beautiful girl, say "Miss New England," in the act of eating, with a delicacy not untinged with avidity, a spoonful of my honey. Besides, it is well known that nothing really sells until everyone wants it at the same time.

All these complicated and yet somehow interesting elements were mirrored in the imperturbability of my merchant.

"Yes, it is good honey," he said, with a damning lack of enthusiasm.

I saw my price going steadily downward. I held up one of the bottles to the light. How I had myself admired its pellucid coloring— how proud had I been of its amber perfection.

"Yes, the color is good," admitted the merchant with a lackluster eye.

Down, down, sank my price.

The only real way, I thought, for a bee-keeper to do is to produce only what he and his family can eat—and then eat it. In that way he can have all the joy of the producer and add to it the disdain of the buyer and the humility of the seller. And why should not the

writer produce only the books he can read—
and then read them: and the musician compose only the music he can play—and then
play it? What a happy world!

When I had just about reached the point of
feeling that I might have to give the merchant
my honey in order to mollify him, he suddenly made a price—oh, he had the art of the
trader!—that was considerably less than I had
hoped, but more than I had begun to expect,
and I closed with him on the spot, and soon
felt the pleasant pressure of money in the
palm of my hand.

It was now that a strange transformation
took place. I began to feel a slightly improved
estimate of human nature, and the lackluster
passivity of the merchant began to relax. After
he had paid over the price and the honey was
no longer mine but his, he took up one of the
beautiful combs, held it up to the light and
looked through it.

"Fine honey," said he with an awakening
glow. "I've not often seen better."

Mr Hyde was swiftly changing there before my eyes into Dr Jekyll. The disdainful
buyer was becoming the eager, the courteous,
the humble seller: he was preparing his spirit

for his new task. As for me, with my money still warm in my hand, I began also to be aware of a swift—and highly pleasant—transformation. As I stepped down the market, I looked about me at the rows of fat cabbages, the sedentary squashes, the boxes of breakfast food, with a kind of disdain, let us say quiet superiority. Just to restore my soul completely I stopped at a counter and with the discriminating, doubtful, slightly hostile air of the careful buyer I asked for a brand of coffee I knew the merchant did not carry. How I reveled in the apologetic deference of the clerk! Here was another brand—famous in every particular. We had considerable amusing, though serious, conversation and, somewhat to my chagrin, when I went out I had a can of the new coffee in my basket. The artful rogue! I carried it home with some presentiment of trouble.

"You *let* him sell it to you," she said.

"Well," I remarked, "we live in a curious world—full of curious people."

"I should think," said she, "that we do."

AUGUST 18. Sudden and considerable honey flow from the goldenrod. All my colonies have been extremely active. In twenty-four hours the bees in my glass hive, which contains only one brood frame, have filled two comb-honey sections, besides much stored below.

So often have I written of the need of quiet —silence: so often quoted Rodin, "Slowness is beauty." Nothing is truer; but I have just come across a passage in Pascal wherein certain of the difficulties are set forth:

"I have often said that all the troubles of man come from his not knowing how to sit still. . . . We combat obstacles in order to get repose, and when we have got it, the repose is insupportable: for we think either of the troubles we have, or of those that threaten us, and even if we felt safe on every side, *ennui* would of its own accord spring up in the depths of the heart where it is rooted by nature, and would fill the mind with its venom."

I seem these days to be inventing epitaphs. Here is one I should like for my own; if I could but deserve it:

"He made inroads upon the infinite."

Spend time every day looking and listening without any ulterior motive whatsoever. Look not as a writer, or as a philosopher, not even as a scientist or an artist—look and listen, simply, like a child, for enjoyment, because the world is interesting and beautiful. Let in nature without the vast and complicated apparatus of duty, ambition, habit, morals, profession—look and listen like a child to the robin in the tree. Of such sights and sounds are the kingdom of beauty, the sources of power and of joy.

I read today an article by one of the best entomologists in America: a man who has spent much of his life experimenting with honeybees.

"We shall never know," he says, "what the world of the bee really is like unless by some miracle of science we become able to see colors which we cannot now see, smell odors which we cannot now smell, and attain other new powers some of which may not even be dreamt of in our present philosophy."

It is true: our ignorance of the bee people is greater than our knowledge.

AUGUST 19. As I sit writing this morning I can hear the shouts, the "haws," the "gees," the "goddams" of the plowman on the south field, plowing in the oat stubble. Sometimes I can hear the creak of his turning plow, subdued by distance into not unmusical notes. I like to hear all this: the distant sound of the busy year. By leaning a little from my small eyrie window I can see his three black horses, one walking in the furrow, two on the stubble. I can see the lazy swishing of their tails; the sun glints upon the clean blade of the upper plow of the sulky. Sometimes the profane plowman rides in his springy iron seat, lifting and swaying with the motion of the plow.

"Back there, ye devils! Whoa now!"

He has dismounted and is walking behind in the furrow. It is a hard pull, angling up the hill, even for a team of three. His pet name for the blacks is profane; he damns them with many a great goddam, yet he is a merciful man, merciful to his beasts. All day they plow thus, transferring the tan-green stubble into the rich dark brown of the soil.

—At noon. I wish you could see them now: the sheer comfort of them, the three blacks standing by the wagon with their noses deep in their oat bags, stamping lazily, swishing their tails to keep off the flies. And the plowman himself, having let the water run until it was cool and drunken his fill, now lies flat on his back in the shade of a spruce tree, his hat drawn down a little and one wrist over his eyes—a picture of complete contentment. I can hear from afar the profanity even of his sleep.

What so many men long for is a place where they can stop thinking, lost in blissful certainty. And there is no such place.

We may rest—and sing—but we must go on.

I have had a sad letter from a man who went to the country to find contentment—and found only more unrest. It is the commonest of mistakes. People seek contentment in places, other places, or expect to find distant neighbors better than those they have near at hand, not knowing that if they are to find contentment, here or there, they must first have the capacity for it in their own souls. For it is inner and not outer. Nevertheless, I know well many cases in which men and women, returning to life in country places, simple living, a certain amount of manual labor (not to exhaustion) and, above all, *stillness,* have been able to reconstruct their lives, even attain an equanimity they have not known before. There is a blessing in the land if a man knows how to kneel for it.

This inventive age! They have so perfected the tea kettle that it no longer sings.

AUGUST 20. The crickets grow more strident as days go by—monotonous and wearisome insect, prophesying fall. One of the few sounds of nature I heartily dislike.

Time clicks out its days, the tireless universe turns, I am caught between two oblivions.

I love books, but compared with John Stuart Mill, who tells in his autobiography (which I have just been enjoying) of the books read in Greek and Latin as well as in English when he was scarce out of swaddling clothes, I feel like a braggart in calling myself a reader at all. But my reading has been a kind of *living,* slow, deep, full of experi-

ence. Not so many books, not so much facts
and history and philosophy, but men and life.
I am a rereader. When I carry a book in my
pocket I carry a man and a friend—as Marcus
Aurelius or Montaigne or Emerson—these so
far as possible to make my familiar companions whom I wish to know and live with.

AUGUST 21. In low spots along old country
roads today I found the joe-pye weed in
bloom: a rank grower, which in mass is often
beautiful. There is a real touch of fall in the
air: at twilight the crickets call. The gold-
finch has a swooping flight: the aristocratic
cedarbirds are through with their late nesting: already the robins are beginning to
gather, restless for their southern journey.
And I found a fringed gentian by a woody
roadside.

The "film of familiarity"—a fine phrase I
find in Munro's translation of Lucretius—ob-
scures many of the glories of life. Beauty is
here, and grandeur, but filmed with familiarity. Dull intimacy! We need a sin or a sorrow to "stab us broad awake." I remember
once, long ago as a boy, stooping over and

looking between my legs at the hills and the rocks of the St Croix. Seen thus upsidedown, how new they were, how surprising, how interesting! For a moment I had broken the film of familiarity. But the sovereign remedy is a more intent gaze, a pause to listen deeply, a moment of insight added to sight.

My lawn-mower man is a philosopher. I enjoy him. He remains a free man in a society of automatons. He is a specialist, but controls his specialty: he knows all there is to know about lawn mowers. He comes with a specially fitted car to gather up sick or enfeebled lawn mowers and takes them to his hospital beyond the hill. A few days later he brings them back, cured. He was here yesterday.

"You can put it over on a man," said he, "but not on a lawn mower. You have to be honest with a lawn mower or it soon tells on you."

"Engineering," says he, "is only a kind of truth."

The failure of a man to be what he might be—to be as great as his capacities would warrant—is not that tragic?

Stay by—life will finally enrich you.

AUGUST 28. These long quiet summer days I
have been much alone. The cicadas rasp the
still air: the birds are silent now, and in the
near woods the squirrels are clipping down
the unripe nuts from the hickory trees. It is
the still middle age of the year: the time of
sunny fullness, of harvest, of fulfillment. I
have been working, writing, thinking. I let
the world go by. Echoes come to me from the
tumult outside, I hear the call to battle, I
do not go. I walk alone across the fields, I
climb Mount Warner and sit in the still
woods, I tramp onward to the wide meadow
above the Hadley ponds and sit there on the
hillside, looking out upon the hazy beauty
of that summer scene—the glint of river, blue
hills beyond, and the shining irregular waters
of the still ponds nearer by—the white steeple
of the church and the roofs of the little town
among the foliage. The tobacco cutters are
at work in the fields below me (I can hear
the high sweet voices of the boys who are slat-
ting the new-cut stalks). It seems to me I
want now to be quiet for a century or so to
consider all the things I have ever seen and

heard and felt and thought. It is not the multiplication of our seeings that increases our lives, but the penetration of them.

Strange, how often ambitious labor, the elaborately planned career, defeats itself, and the rewards are heaped upon the man of joy —who has already had his reward. There is no justice under the sun!

Wanted: more noble men in little places.

Long ago I made up my mind to let my friends have their peculiarities.

Emerson tells in his journal of an aunt of his who had a "fatal gift of penetration." "She disgusted everybody because she knew them too well."

AUGUST 30. I felt as much complimented today as though I had been praised for writing a good book: a man I met, who had bought a comb of my honey from my friend, the market man, told me he thought it as fine honey as ever he ate in his life. I knew he was right: I am not always so sure of those who praise my books. The market man seems a fairly good publisher of my honey: he devises excellent blurbs and sees that the likeliest reviewers have the first taste. He knows also that success depends as much upon mouth-to-mouth commendation as upon advertising; and unlike some publishers he is ready with a new edition before the old one is exhausted.

SEPTEMBER

IN THE COUNTRYMAN'S YEAR

"That statement only is fit to be made public which you have come at in attempting to satisfy your own curiosity."—EMERSON, *Spiritual Laws.*

CHAPTER VI

SEPTEMBER IN THE COUNTRYMAN'S YEAR

SEPTEMBER 2. What a good time of the year is this. The fat land! I spent much of the afternoon and evening gathering peaches, plums and pears, some as fine as ever I saw —ripe from the trees. I brought in a large sample basket containing the best of the Carman peaches (white-fleshed), ripe Bartlett pears, purple plums, bunches of grapes

(Moore's Early and small sweet Niagaras), a few McIntosh apples (drops, for the crop is not ready) and two fine muskmelons. It was a sight to see. We have now also an abundance of most excellent tomatoes, sweet corn and lima beans. A good time of year: the fat land!

The other day I thought I would take my little book out to the hives with me and write down, just as they came to me, certain of my thoughts and observations. I put the book and the pen on the smooth top of one of the hives, where I could easily turn to them as I was at work elsewhere. And these are the notes I set down:

In the hive no bee obeys any other bee.

No bee commands or tries to command any other bee, except possibly in driving out the drones in September, though this is communal, not individual.

No bee ever amasses anything for himself or asks anything that all other bees cannot have on the same terms.

No bee ever creates anything new or preserves anything old. For inconceivable millions of years (we know from the Baltic fossils) there has never been any change, or any evolution, not even any degeneration. Endless repetition: a living machine; the very thought of which is a great weariness.

Unlike man, no bee ever has any secret or individual life.

The life of the hive rests not upon obedience to bee persons, not even the queen, as old observers steeped in monarchical ideas so easily concluded, but to bee law—an unchangeable, heartless, mindless foreordination.

There are certain limited freedoms for the bee that men have never yet achieved. A bee eats, but never overeats, from the common store. It eats when and how it pleases, works when and how it pleases, apparently at such tasks as it pleases; it crawls into a cell or hangs up to the comb to sleep when weary. There are no matins or curfews in any colony.

Such things as illness, injuries, the decrepitude of age are sternly dealt with by the bee society: weakness or defectiveness means death. Pity is nonexistent.

The bee has senses that man does not know. Are the things it sees, smells, hears, feels, therefore less natural?

The hive has the principle of self-sacrificing

unity developed to perfection: any bee will instantly give up its life for the safety of the swarm.

The bee has settled, so far as its own evolution is concerned, one of the most difficult of the problems of life—that of sex. It has staked the entire possibility of survival in a single bee—the queen. This is what makes bee breeding so difficult. It is conservatism driven to the last degree.

Man has risen, or changed, because he could, however slightly, modify natural law, or use law for his own creative purposes. The bee is at a dead end of its development because of its overdevotion to the centripetal principle of life. Man has preserved the balance between unity and diversity—the often dangerous balance. It is exciting to be a man!

If man could consign to unity some of the elements of his life now torn by diversity, which he seems determined to do, he might well be happier, but would he be more creative?

As I am to the bee, so may there be intelligences in the universe far superior to me. As I guide, following the Law, is it possible that I may be guided? How often, working with my bees of a sunny morning among the apple trees, have I had the sense, deeper than sense, of being somehow worked with, somehow used, somehow guided.

SEPTEMBER 8. Rain, fog, clouds, gloom. Not a breath of air stirring. The wet brown leaves of the elms eddy straight downward, covering the wheel tracks in the road. Every leaf of the hemlock holds a pendent drop: there are no bird notes: the bees keep safe at home. A drab worker or two in the onion fields, silent and slow, defies the weather. Two crows I saw drifting heavily across the melancholy sky. I, a cowled monk, withdraw into myself, and reflect upon life and death.

SEPTEMBER 9. Another day of fog. Fog in our valley, fog in the country at large, fog in the whole world. Each asks the way of the other: no one knows where he is, or which way to go. Never in my time have I known the like of it. The old system we knew and have lived under seems breaking down, shaking political institutions to their depths.

To be made happy by the sight of a song sparrow on a hemlock bough—all of its little flashing graceful movements—that is something!

Give me *this* day. I am skeptical of tomorrow: will there be one?

I think often and with encouragement of Paul Bourget's way of letting his books come out, each one a disappointment to him (as mine are to me), but with the comforting reflection that the deficiencies of one book can be cured in the next! If it were not for his next book—his great and beautiful next book —could any writer go on?

SEPTEMBER 10. Today I watched several of my bee colonies at the annual holocaust of the drones: one of the exciting events of the year. All summer these great lumbering male bees have been nurtured by the workers, an easy and comfortable existence, plenty of food and warmth, and no labor. In every hive there is always a large superfluity—nature providing generously, as always, for the perpetuation of the species. Scores and even hundreds are maintained that three or four during the summer—sometimes only one—may perform the indispensable function of impregnating a new queen. But with the coolness of autumn coming on, and new supplies of honey no longer available, the thrifty commune slaughters every drone in the hive. Between September and the following May, in this climate, there is no male element in any of the colonies. A hint at what a really organized and efficient society may become!

I watched the bumbling old fellows come rolling out of the hive with two or three workers biting fiercely at them, pushing, pulling, dragging—tumbling them finally off the landing board into the grass. The drones are individually much stronger than the workers and shake them off repeatedly, sometimes rising into the air with a worker clinging to their legs. Again and again they return hopefully to the hive, trying to dodge their way back into the only home they have ever known, only to have the workers set upon them with new ferocity, until they are worn out or starved out and drop helpless in the grass, to be eaten by skunks, or birds, or ants, or wasps. Apparently the worker never uses its sting, and the drone, having none, is quite defenseless. It seems a merciless and wasteful process, and yet it is nature's immutable method, nature's economy, approved by the continued survival of one of the most ancient of living societies.

Should one pity the results of the iron working of natural law?

So much of human sympathy is soft, toothless—wasted upon the inevitable. At the same time so much that is really pitiable—to wring the souls of men—since it can be changed, is smudged over, unseen, unassuaged. What the world needs is not new sight but new insight.

Happiness and enjoyment are quite different. Happiness has in it something carefree, childish, naïve. It is simple, free, transitory. But one may enjoy, and enjoy the more deeply, for having known suffering, tasted sorrow. Enjoyment is complex and increases with knowledge and experience.

Most people, looking, see nothing: others have only to turn their heads, and lo!—wonders!

I have been reading a new biography (by Routh) of Sir Thomas More. It is like certain tasteless puddings I have known in which, however, the plums of quotation, all delicious, are so generously stirred in that the product is appetizing. The quaint narrative of Roper, More's son-in-law, is still the best for giving one an intimate view.

I love this man: the playfulness combined with deep earnestness of character: love with discipline: dreams with practical wisdom, courage, steadfastness—and such graces of mind and spirit! Charm without surrender!

It so happens that I have been with him in this book not so long after a sojourn with that angular American, Thoreau. In the essential principles of their lives these two would find themselves much in accord—but how different in *manners!* After associating with this noble and courteous knight, how thin, narrow, cold, appears the sage of Walden Pond. King Henry, walking with More, was wont to throw his arm over his friend's shoulder: Emerson said that he would as soon think of taking the arm of an elm tree as that of Henry Thoreau.

More dreamed well his Utopia, but deep down he knew that it was "impossible that all should be well, unless all men are good, which I do not expect for many years to come."

He loved simple things. He would have

nothing that could not "be gathered all times of the year in the garden of thine own soul." He would have "no strange thing therein, nothing costly to buy, nothing far to fetch."

All simple, normal, all in one's own soul. No strange thing, nothing far to fetch!

He knew, no one better, what he wanted to do: he longed for perfection, but he was willing to be patient in meeting the obstacles in the way of reaching it. In the end he too lost his head.

SEPTEMBER 13. Now the bees are active on goldenrod and aster: the swift going and coming, the comfortable hum of bountiful production.

I brought in from the garden another large basket of ripe muskmelons. We have this year a good crop, the flesh a salmon pink in color, excellent and sweet. The third planting of Golden Bantam corn is now at its best, cheating the early frost, as I had hoped. In the orchard a scent of ripening pears: I pass a McIntosh apple tree to gather one to eat and one for my pocket in case I should meet a likely boy.

Days pass, I do nothing.

My good friend Waugh has an infallible cure for political digust.

"Asters," says he, "are always delightful and interesting, but in a political campaign they are indispensable. When one is thoroughly disgusted reading political speeches he can always go out and look at the asters and feel better."

There is something in the Hindu belief. I myself hate to stop the life of anything that lives: I cannot start it again. I step devoutly among these moving marvels.

"It is not miserable to be blind; it is miserable to be incapable of enduring blindness." This was the high spirit in which John Milton met his limitation (I find it in his *Second Defense of the People of England*). Good Aurelian philosophy!

SEPTEMBER 15. We have a Polish family on a small farm just below us in the valley. They built a house a few years ago out of an old barn, adding scraps of lumber, doors, bits of railing, even packing boxes, picked up for a song in the town. We have seen them literally expanding under our eyes. Last winter and spring the man completed a tobacco shed: we heard him hammering and sawing at dawn before we were up, and sometimes late at night we could see the flickering light of his lantern as he perched on the roof, nailing down the last of the shingles. He did it all himself. I walked down through the fields today where he is cutting the rowen crop of his alfalfa. His wife was there with him, barelegged, bareheaded, sunburned, working like a man. His young son, whose legs were scarcely long enough to reach the clutch, was driving the hay rake. A vigorous and cheerful-looking family! The man works with an eager, quick swing of his arms and legs as though he enjoyed it. The woman looks up with a smile on her face. We commented on the fact that his neighbors, the P——s, who are Americans of the proud old stock, are selling out: auction next Thursday.

"He say," observed my Pole with a broad smile, "he say too much work, no money."

This seems everywhere the process: the old stock, demanding higher standards of living and of education, surrendering the land to these thrifty and energetic Polish people.

Today, I said, I have wasted my time. How do I know? When one lives deeply, is time wasted?

I read this today in the 113th Psalm:
"Who *humbleth* himself to behold the things that are in the heaven, and in the earth."

For the price of a bowl of soup I bought today at an old bookshop a volume to me infinitely valuable—a boon, a prize, a priceless possession. All the way home on the train I read it: I was enlarged, I acquired merit, I added to my life.

SEPTEMBER 16. Tragedy! A yellow-billed cuckoo flew full force against my window and was instantly killed. A tuft of white down left on the glass showed where she met her death. A fine bird, measuring a foot from tip of bill to tip of tail, one we rarely see here, possibly because it is really scarce, and possibly because it is a shy bird, keeping to the thickets. It has little personality, and its song or squawk is not pleasing.

A mellow day. I picked the last of the yellow Elberta peaches.

What dreary reading the newspapers these days: such violence, crime, greed, fear, suspicion—a bitter and evil and unreasoning world here incontinently disclosed. In this day's paper—I looked, carefully—I found almost nothing, certainly not more than half a dozen items, to nourish a man's courage or hope, stimulate his love of beauty, awaken in him a new devotion to truth. How can such a world, if this is a true exemplification of it —which I do not believe—avoid a speedy explosion?

I have taken this inestimable gift of life too casually: its "elves of hills, brooks, standing lakes, and groves": mornings and evenings, sunshine and rain: family, friends, town. I have been dully ungrateful. I might never have been here at all!

SEPTEMBER 17. Mornings like this, it seems, there is nothing that is not possible: nothing I do not believe. I look about the earth and the heavens: there is not *enough* to believe— mornings like this.

"A wayfaring tree." For many years we have had several varieties of viburnum growing near us, a delightful and beautiful shrub: but I found how ignorant I really was of its many virtues until I ran across, in Evelyn's dull diary, a reference to it as "a wayfaring tree"—a fine name if ever there was one. In reading the description that followed I learned that we had been harboring unaware, in our common garden, a shrub of many distinctions.

"The viburnum," he says, "or wayfaring tree, growing plentifully in every corner, makes pins for the yokes of oxen; and superstitious people think that it protects their cattle from being bewitched and place the shrub about their stalls; it certainly makes the most pliant and best bands to fagot with. The leaves and berries are astringent, and make an excellent gargle for loose teeth, sore throat, and stop fluxes. The leaves decocted to a lye not only color the hair black but fasten the roots; and the bark of the root macerated underground, well beaten, and often boiled, serves for bird lime."

The next time I go into my garden I shall take off my hat and make a low bow to *viburnum opulus*.

SEPTEMBER. SUNDAY. Dull and cloudy all day long. We went to Butter Hill to call on our friends the Cutlers. At the entrance to their grounds a fine bush of the black alder full of red berries, notable to see. Never such rock walls as these on old roads on Pelham hill. I recall the remark of our old friend Robinson, who loved New England to the point of writing a book about its beautiful old doorways, that more labor had gone into the stone walls of Massachusetts than into the pyramids of Egypt. Free labor, too!

Autumn coloring is beginning to show. The elms grow rusty, and the nut trees, but the clematis blooms white by the wall, asters and goldenrod color the countryside, last fading proof of summer.

There is such a thing—I have heard of it —as living too long or too much. I do not believe it.

It is settled: there is no time. Everything, always, is now. There is no space: everything is here.

Nor have I any faith in numbers—or in majorities—or in crowds.

You will go by, in coming years, you will
go by and never know that I was here: that
here in this sunny field upon this hillside I
fought Apollyon; that I was hot and hard
and evil here, I was possessive and passionate
here; I saw beauty here, and loved here; here
I won, finally, a great victory, established the
state of my own soul, made laws and obeyed
them, and at last sat here, quite still, looking
out upon the beauty of my hills.—You will
go by, and I shall not be here.

SEPTEMBER 21. The earliest autumn coloring
along the country roads comes on woodbine
and poison ivy, except here and there a fiery
maple bough. The cornflower is in bloom, the
goldenrod is passing, the asters are at the
height of their glory. In our garden the chrys-
anthemums are just coming out.

SEPTEMBER 25. Never, I think, have I seen
the summer so deepen into maturity, such
autumn days—such serenity—such placid
beauty—never as this year. But it has a sadness.

I should like in future years to be a little
remembered.

SEPTEMBER 26. My desk in the forenoons, daily labor to weariness; my garden and bees in the afternoons, and many friends in and out. A life that should be wholly satisfactory, if there were only more time for the lift and ease of the spirit. The autumn comes now, full of beauty, no killing frost at all, but warm, still, sunny days and cool nights full of peace. The apples are falling, the luscious Washington plums, as large as peaches, hang yellow-ripe on the tree, the early pears are in and canned, the late Clapps I shall be gathering today. We have a world of grapes, and the melons are the best that ever I raised in my life. This year I tried a new variety called the Bender, which does better here than any other.

In the evening I am reading the annals of Rome in Gibbon's *Decline and Fall*—a book full of sanguinary but not unpleasant atrocities. So the days click by and scarcely leave a trace.

SEPTEMBER 27. This morning white frost on the grass, first of the season, causing no damage even to the most delicate foliage. Our hillside, with excellent air drainage, is the last place in town to be touched by such severities.

SEPTEMBER 29. Innumerable spider webs on the morning grass prophesied correctly, and by noon the fog had burned off and the day was hot and bright. The robins are flocking, ready for their journey southward.

This evening excellent music.

I know a man who went through the battle of Belleau Wood, saw bloody, terrible things, saw a soldier's head shot off, was hungry, thirsty, terror-stricken—yet came away bringing nothing, without a mark upon his essential personality. He had nothing to experience with.

SEPTEMBER 30. It is the time when the provident must defend their laborious savings: today I watched numerous small wild bees with gold and black abdomens, which, having scented the rich stores of honey in the hives, were trying to steal their way through the guarded entrance. They had, actually, the furtive air of sneak thieves. Each time, however, they were set upon and driven off, though not without an obstinate struggle. I saw one thing, a grisly evidence of the ruthlessness of nature, that I had never seen before. Two or three of these savage wild bees, hovering hungrily near the entrance of a hive, discovered one of the drones which the workers are now driving out. They pounced upon the poor old fellow and literally tore the head off the living but enfeebled body, and afterwards began sucking at the contents of both head and body. A savage business! I imagined what a horrible and shocking thing it would have been if these bees in the grass had been suddenly enlarged to the size of men, or else I, their gigantic spectator, reduced to their own size.

I am uniting some of my weaker colonies so that I shall not have so many to carry through the winter.

OCTOBER

IN THE COUNTRYMAN'S YEAR

Johnson: "There is nothing, Sir, too little for so little a creature as man. It is by studying little things that we attain the great art of having as little misery and as much happiness as possible."—BOSWELL, *Volume I.*

CHAPTER VII

OCTOBER IN THE COUNTRYMAN'S YEAR

OCTOBER 1. We have had two days of a wild
southeaster, hills smothered with mist, warm
rain whipping down the corn, shaking off the
apples, covering all the ground under the pine
trees with a thick brown carpet of fallen
needles. I like well to be out in a "souther."
There is a transport of abandonment about it,

a reckless inconstancy, one moment a gushing, smothering downpour of rain, all passion and ardor, the next a sweet lassitude when soft white mists, like snowy arms, envelop the wayfarer, and even, at moments, the sun glancing from behind heavy-lidded clouds. Strange are the moods of such days as these, a wild, dear fickleness.

The "souther" is rare with us. Our common storms are from the northwest: stern, gray, puritan storms, with sharp rain and cutting winds—but the "souther"!

After a "souther" at this time of year the weather commonly turns cool and we have a day—like this—of indescribable clearness and brightness, all the murkiness gone, all the earth washed clean, and the sun shining in an absolutely cloudless sky.

The farmer likes the "souther" not at all, for it shakes down his fruit before he can pick it, lodges his corn before he can cut it, blows in at the south windows of his hayloft which he has left trustfully open. And no storms we have twist off so many old trees or bring down so many weakened branches. The forests are well prepared for the businesslike western and northern storms, keep well pruned to meet them, but when one of these beguiling, reckless, smothering "southers" appears, the old habited trees, taken quite by surprise, are easy victims.

When I was a boy I learned much, Sunday evenings, lying full on the bed with my father, he with his lamp at his elbow, reading aloud the old wild Norse legends of Odin and Thor— I learned the Deception of Appearance, Thor drinking all unknowing from the horn of the gods and draining the sea; or wrestling with the old woman who was Time. Nothing was what it seemed: everything was something else.

If you see a man slow in a crowd, guess that I am that man.

Love is not difficult if we begin by giving it.

After all, the great books, many of them, have been small books, lean with essentials— Bacon's *Essays,* Marcus Aurelius, William Penn's *Solitude,* Pascal's *Thoughts,* the Book of Job, Jonson's *Timber.*

OCTOBER 3. I am beginning to get my bee colonies ready for the long winter. Some of them are short of stores, and I have been feeding back all the half-filled frames, ragged combs and uncapped honey that seems too immature to keep. I use an empty super placed on top of the hive which protects the colony while it is at work. The bees go at the unexpected treasures as though famished, and in one night will take downstairs and store in their own frames an astonishing amount of honey. They leave every comb as clean as though it were new, every cell empty and polished. The only difficulty in these cool days, when there is so little nectar to be had outside, is that the entire apiary, once it gets a whiff of uncapped stores, will become excited, and if the beekeeper does not move deftly and get his supplies quickly into the feeding supers, he will have a first-class riot on his hands. All the good, honest, hard-working citizens of these peaceful commonwealths, lured by unexpected riches, will begin robbing one another like Apache Indians. Even after the honey is shut into a tight feeding-super, bees from other colonies will pry about the cracks and generally make nuisances of themselves.

I am also having my bees, the tidiest of

housekeepers, clean up all the old honey cans and jars, as well as the extractor: they can do it far better than I can and at the same time increase their stores. A little later, if any colony is still deficient, I shall feed it with thick sugar syrup, for the secret of good wintering is an abundance of food.

In the morning newspaper I find, apt to my thinking, the report of an address at Venice by Guglielmo Marconi, surely one of the most distinguished of living scientists and inventors. "Science," he says, "has absolutely failed to explain the problem of life. . . . We succeed only in creating outlines and translating a measure into numbers without our minds being able to form any concrete idea of it."

And he concludes that man, "who wishes to explain the tormenting mystery," is confronted by "a book closed with seven seals."

How well I remember, years ago at college, listening to A. R. Wallace, the co-discoverer with Darwin of the principle of evolution, lecture on "The Wonderful Century." I remember with what vivid enthusiasm, what certainty, I accepted the faith, so deeply held by those great prophets and precursors, that science was destined, in no long time, to solve the mystery of the universe, unlock the door of human fate. To my brave brother, who sat near me on that memorable evening so long ago, science became, literally, a religion to which he devoted his life with utter singleness of purpose, for which finally he died.

And *now* the greatest of scientists—not Marconi alone—are plagued more than ever before by the old "tormenting mystery." Every discovery they make reveals, just beyond, illimitable new worlds for exploration: every end unfolds myriad beginnings.

It was a great age: the age of faith in science. I was there: I lived through it: I felt it. I know well what it means to believe that the Explanation lies just around the near corner, beyond the next hill. "About the secret—quick about it, Friend!"

How completely is that early ardor spent. How weary the sense among scientists of unending toil to penetrate even a little way into the jungle of the unknown.

The world labors in a time of tired faith: there is as yet no new ardor to take the place of the old. The intellect of man seems not sufficient: not mathematics, not physics, not chemistry, not psychology. The Lord is not in the wind, nor yet in the earthquake, nor yet in the fire.

OCTOBER 4. Winey autumn mornings, clear and bright and still. I have just come in from a tramp in country roads, to look at the new world.

Mornings I like best. Breakfast is altogether the best meal of the day. I like breakfast! Half a Bender melon from our own garden, rich golden yellow, ripe and sweet; a hot wheat biscuit upon which I spread a broad slice of my own comb honey, fresh from the hive, delicious to the taste. Upon this I pour a generous libation of my neighbor Kentfield's good milk. Black coffee, fresh-made, with sugar but no cream, two slices of toast and a rasher of bacon—what could be better? I come to it eager every morning and think I could devise nothing better to start the day. After that, a tramp down Hadley road, or around the square, and I am back at my desk—as at this moment—ready to harness Pegasus to the lumber wagon of my daily labor.

How capricious thought is—backing and filling, running off the straight track, stopping to look at the flowers or listen to the birds, lying down to rest under many an ambrosial apple tree of the imagination, having moments of utter discouragement because everything has already been written down in books —and, springing up one morning, like this, to go forward again, full of the joy of discovery.

So many people have undeveloped powers of enjoyment: it is sad they do not know it.

What enormous folly!—that there can be only one party in a state: one set of ideas: one religion. Yet dictators rest their case upon this fallacy. As well a stick with one end: a magnet with one pole.

One comes at length to wear himself like an old shoe: you can see how comfortable he is by the look in his eye.

We have a neighbor who has tremendous enjoyment spending money she does not possess and never will possess. Her house is over-furnished in every room with unbought chairs, rugs, beds, tables, books, china. She even has two cocker spaniels running about in her living room, giving her no trouble at all because they are imaginary.

OCTOBER 5. Now these are the joys of October days: the red of ivy upon the wall, and purple asters all in bloom; grapes in heavy clusters among their frosted leaves; and in the distant swamps the maples red and yellow.

A dog barks from the farm below, I can hear a song sparrow among the purple-leaved barberries, and bees humming in the still sunshine.

I rest here upon this hillside. There is a haze upon the western hills. Distant farm roofs gleam. The smoke from a chimney rises straight into the quiet air. Far away are cities, and far the troubled world.

Having at length accepted my place in the universe: mine and no other: I grow quiet, like my hemlock tree; tranquil, like my elm.

I love well to follow up (better than follow down) a hill stream, and have been at one I know now at various times for a week or so, beginning each day where I left off the day before. Going up, one comes always to more rugged scenery, wilder hills, where the stream, which lower in the valley loafs in fat fields, is alive with youth, leaps down the rocky hillsides, sings at its play. Sometime I will write a biography of this stream, describe all the bridges it flashes under, all the wheels it turns, all the still ponds it lingers in, and how the cattle in a hundred meadows come down to drink at its rushy margins, or wade in its sunny shallows; how at length, slipping out tranquilly, it finds peace in the broad bosom of the Connecticut River.

OCTOBER 8. Cool sharp mornings, inconceivably beautiful. I began picking my Baldwin apples. High up in one of the trees I felt vainglorious enough, remembering how, only a few minutes ago (or so it seems), I set out that very tree, a frail sapling, with my own hands. I have seen it grow, pruned it, sprayed it, and am now reaping the rich fruit of it. This gives a kind of satisfaction that one can get, I think, in no other way.

Life brought me here: life uses me: life will care for me when I am through. Why so hot, little soul? With all your care you cannot change a single letter of the law, nor alter a line of the ultimate decree.

How much good time and energy we waste in trying to change the past: time that we might use in changing the present—and future.

I know a woman who employs a good part of her waking hours holding post-mortems.

Shepard, whom I met today, said he was as busy as a cat on a tin roof. Last time I met him he was even busier: as busy as a dog with two tails.

OCTOBER 9. Elaborate loafing, of which I am ashamed—and enjoy!

Men are husking corn in my neighbor's field: a good sight to see.

Come now to my hillside and be still. It is only a little way to understanding if you will be still, only a little way to peace.

No book that does not somehow give us the sense of a possessed soul will last.

I know a man reads as many books as any other in this town—good books, too—but they seem to do nothing to him, or for him. It reminds me of a comment my neighbor S—— made on one of our common acquaintances who died recently—as cadaverous a human being as ever I saw.

"He et and he et," said S——, "but it didn't do him no good. He didn't get no fatter."

OCTOBER 10. A perfect autumn day: New England at its best. I wish I could look long enough at the coloring on Mount Warner to keep it permanently in my inner eye. Such a tapestry of beauty: such sunlight: such crystal air! Was there ever anything finer? But if I could really retain it all, I might grow slothful with contentment, and another autumn, other golden and red tapestries, the wine of other Octobers, might fall upon a surfeited spirit.

It is enough: *today* I am alive.

"Lo, these are parts of His ways: but how little a portion is heard of Him?—but the thunder of His power who can understand?"

"In the course of generations . . . men will excuse you for not doing as they do, if you will bring enough to pass in your own way."

This I ran across in Thoreau's *Journals,* on page 313, and have thought of it with encouragement.

OCTOBER 11. First hard frost, all the meadows white with it, glistening in the morning sun. A perfect autumn morning, I delight in. The glory of the maples is passing, the glory of the oaks not fully here.

I found one of my apple trees full of starlings and stood watching them for a long time, listening to their delightful private conversation, interrupted from time to time by ironic whistling, no doubt at the enormity of the gossip that was going around. Some there are who dislike starlings, consider them nuisances, not without some cause, but few birds I know are more interesting to me than they are.

I love best healthy normal things. I like to see things going on, just as they are. I know a man rushes to see a two-headed calf or a five-legged sheep. I prefer a good healthy one-headed calf; and I like my sheep with four legs. What I like best rarely gets in any newspaper.

I read today an interview with the famous scientist Einstein saying that he didn't care what political creed the world adopts "if it brings happiness to the human race."

"It's happiness we're after," said he.

But no creed or system will ever bring happiness. Happy men—if I know what happiness is—are not dependent upon a political creed or an economic system. There have been happy men and good men in all ages, under all governments: there have been miserably unhappy men under the best we know. Men generally never had more comforts, luxuries, larger freedoms and opportunities than they have today—but what vast unhappiness and discontent! I quote again and again lines from Goldsmith's *Traveller* I learned long ago:

"How small of all that human hearts endure
 The part that kings and laws can cause or
  cure."

If Einstein is happy, and I suspect he is, in large measure, it is dependent upon no outward creed or system.

OCTOBER 12. It is the bluebird time of year: I saw a large flock yesterday in Pelham. Stately pheasants come up in the early morning to feed in our meadow. The open warm spaces are sporting fields for millions of crickets: wasps light on the sunny window sill of my study. The ash leaves are falling fast, and there are broad splashes of red and gold in the swamp and on the shoulders of Mount Warner. And the tingling air is full of sunshine.

Life goes hard with the prophets! Long ago, when such prophecies pleased me, I read —and copied out—lines from Victor Hugo:

"In the twentieth century war will be dead, the scaffold will be dead, hatred will be dead, frontier boundaries will be dead, dogmas will be dead: man will live."

And here we are in the twentieth century!

OCTOBER 13. Hermit thrushes at our window feeding on the purple woodbine berries. A true comely bird, usually shy here and seldom seen, but now, no doubt, migrating. I picked two barrels of excellent Baldwin and Northern Spy apples.

These autumn days are beyond adjectives: every adjective I know seems leaden-footed when applied to mornings like these, or trusted to reveal the secret inner meaning of the hills, or interpret the message of the trees. I need verbs! Verbs to show what days like these *do* to a man's soul.

OCTFBER 15. We have now a world of grapes. I think a man could stand all day long eating them with no harm done. Once long ago in Italy I heard of what they called the "grape cure." Pompous, puffy old politicians and bankers, who have attended too many banquets and acquired gout and a paunch, betake themselves to idyllic hillsides in Tuscany when the soft airs of Italy are most beguiling, and the vineyards are at their best, and for days on end eat nothing whatever but grapes, ripe and fresh from the vines. Miraculous cures are reported.

I can well believe it. One of these falls I'll make my fortune by posting an advertisement, say in the Bankers' Club in New York, and the Senate lounge at Washington, inviting the entire membership to my hillside in Amherst. I'll provide easy chairs and even umbrellas by my arbors and let them eat grapes all day long. And once in twenty-four hours I'll appear and lecture them well on the danger of having too much money. I shall thus prepare them for going back home and making more money than ever before.

How can a man live fully, enjoy deeply, if half or more of his mind is clogged with fear?

I think, these days, I shall never again be serious, or write large dull books: I shall spend my hours walking about and laughing at all the curious things I see.

This gluttony for ceaseless action! Be still, be still!

OCTOBER 16. I have been for a long tramp in country roads and with a kind of joy I cannot quite explain, since I heard nothing that could be sung on any stage, nor saw anything that could be published in any paper. An old man in his field digging mangels, lifting and bending there, all gray in the sunshine, I stopped to talk with. A man currying a horse in a sunny barnyard and whistling as he worked. A woman sitting flat in the field swiftly topping onions. Three men with an ox team (we still have ox teams in New England) hauling a great load of wood out of the forest. Boys husking corn. A man up a tall ladder picking apples. Fat bags of onions in long rows, tobacco hanging brown in open sheds, squashes and pumpkins piled high on sunny porches. Cows in the wide meadows. An enormous pig rooting in a potato field with unbounded unction, comfort, physical satisfaction in every grunt. I stopped there to laugh at him.

Why should all these simple things so delight me?

How easily accessible the really great rewards of life! One has only to step up and take them.

OCTOBER 22. Now come sunny mornings, cool and still, when the leaves drift downward through the sparkling air. No wind stirs them, no frost, no rain: it is the serene culmination of life. They go in beauty. On such a day I can bear anything!

Can you be simple, true, genuine, in any environment—an attic, a mountain top, a palace? Second-rate poets, prophets, saints put on something outside: a painter at Provincetown has painted the door of his house yellow and the blinds blue to let us know he is an artist: a poet seeks a symbolic attic, a saint a cell, a scholar a degree. But how easily Marcus Aurelius wore his palace and Epictetus his slavery. Badges are for men not great enough in themselves.

OCTOBER 25. A drizzling, black, chill morning with flurries of snow—the first of the year. Everywhere falling leaves and somber bare trees. When I went out at noon I heard from the woods the crack of a hunter's gun. One takes out of life only what he puts into it in imagination.

I delight in my road talks with my friend and neighbor, Brown. He has a husky kind of humor. Meeting yesterday, we discussed several things with some warmth.

"Fact is," said he finally, "I don't know much about politics. Beyond M, I am ignorant."

"Beyond M?" I asked. "What do you mean?"

"Well, you see," said he, "my Encyclopaedia Britannica ends at M."

He told me he had bought from a defaulting subscriber all the volumes up to M for three dollars. He was looking for another defaulting subscriber who had the volumes from N onward.

"If I get them," said he, "perhaps I'll learn something about politics."

OCTOBER 26. A golden autumn afternoon, of a polished stillness and calm beauty. I visited B——'s cider mill at the top of his orchard. He was at work pouring the small ripe Baldwin apples into the hopper. Not one was wormy, not one rotten, for B—— is honest with his cider. I saw the pulp fall into the frames on the cheese block, saw it wrapped with the coarse brown expression cloth—five layers, one above the other. I saw the motor turned on and the slow upward thrust of the irresistible oil plunger—three thousand pounds of pressure. I saw the rich yellow juice pouring out of the cheese and held a glass, and drank it there, as fine and clean a draft as ever I tasted—the natural sweet essence of our New England hills. B—— tells me he gets about three and a half gallons to a bushel of apples. I saw the plunger released, the expression cloths opened, and the dry brown pomace emptied out. B—— feeds it sparingly to his cows, says it is as good as silage. A rotary strainer removes the last fragments of the apple pulp and leaves the liquid clear as amber. It is then decanted into gallon jugs and sold on merit in the town. When I left, B—— insisted upon presenting me with one of the jugs to take home, and I, on my part, having some of my honey in the car, presented him with a good comb, which he was delighted to have. It was a pleasant experience.

I was sad: the world seemed hard and bleak. I stopped in the evening to look at a brown hill, brown with autumn, mirrored in a little lake. A young moon hung in the sky. Somewhere, far off, I heard the cattle calling. A little cool-scented breeze touched my face—and suddenly I was at peace, standing still there.

OCTOBER 27. Cold, raw days. After the frost and the rain the countryside has lost the gaiety of its coloring, has become somber in browns, tans, grays.

I have been extracting the last of my honey. I use a hand-driven, two-frame extractor which does excellent work. I have filled all the jars I bought and all I could find around the house. The color is not as good as last year, since there is a considerable mixture of darker honey—partly buckwheat—but the flavor, so far as I can see, is equally fine. I have had some attractive labels printed bearing my name and address.

NOVEMBER

IN THE COUNTRYMAN'S YEAR

"For thou shalt be in league with the stones of the field; and the beasts of the field shall be at peace with thee."—THE BOOK OF JOB.

CHAPTER VIII

NOVEMBER IN THE COUNTRYMAN'S YEAR

NOVEMBER 1. Yesterday, being a gloomy day, I paid my taxes.

That strange shrub, the witch hazel, is now in full bloom, defying winter.

NOVEMBER 3. A good day in the country; one of those still, sunny, New England autumn days when one is glad of being alive. I worked at the pruning of my grapevines and began on the Baldwin apple trees. It was so cold, at first, that I wore my old overcoat and thick gloves, but by the middle of the afternoon the sun shone warm, and the bees were flying from the hives in the orchard, a pleasant, sonorous hum I like to hear. Next week I shall be putting away the colonies in their winter boxes. While I was at work a flock of chewinks, the first I have seen, came to rest in the hedge, quite sociable and saucy, and later, just at evening, two heavy, weary-looking crows flew over, high up.

All day Thomisky, the teamster, has been at work in my meadow and orchard, a man of true native force and excellent judgment. I like to hear him shout at his horses. I like to see the loaded wagon creaking up the hill. He is clearing the last weathered corn shocks from the cornfield.

At noon Thomisky drove his wagon behind the big spruce, unhooked the traces and tethered his horses to one of the wheels. I watched him shake out a bundle of hay for the noon feeding; oats, too, a good allowance, spread out on gunny sacks on the floor of the wagon. He blanketed both horses, strapping the cloth under their bellies to keep them warm after the long forenoon of heavy work. It was fine to see them there, quite comfortable in the

sunshine, munching their oats. Thomisky himself put on his sheep-lined jacket and sat on
the wagon boards with his lunch bucket between his knees, eating great hunks of bread
and sausage and onions, quite as placid as his
horses. When he had finished, a kind of stillness settled down upon him: rest and comfort
after labor. He has a singularly serene face.

I like such days as these, good quiet days,
simple things.

It was dark when I came in, and I was
tired. I smelled the supper cooking as soon
as I opened the door—surely one of the good
moments of life.

Afterwards I spent the evening reading in
bed. I have a good light on the table near my
left shoulder, little scraps of paper to write
on, a pen and pencils: and a pile of my necessary and favorite books. I prop my head up
on the pillows and, on cool nights like these,
slip my arms into an old warm dressing gown
the collar of which fits snugly around my neck
and shoulders. And there I lie in the quiet
room and read and read and read—and think
how much men of old times were like ourselves; how we repeat the same foolish mistakes, suffer the same sorrows, enjoy the same

pleasant things; and how we hope to know more and live better—and never do.

I think most people run after things not worth having: a man can be richest who chooses what others leave.

We are so little deserving of paradises. The old story infinitely repeats itself. Given paradises, an angel with a flaming sword is forever driving us out of them. Given opportunity, beauty, leisure, power, how easily and swiftly we befoul them.

I wish some of the ardent advisers of the human race would read a certain passage in Liber I of Thomas à Kempis:

"Be not angry that you cannot make others as you wish them to be since you cannot make yourself as you wish to be."

NOVEMBER 4. I know why English gardeners speak of "lifting" their turnips. It is far more expressive than "harvesting." There is a bent back in the picture! Today I lifted the roots of the witloof chicory I have been nursing for the bitter winter salad we like so well. I wonder why more gardeners do not propagate it. Nothing is easier. It is planted like parsnips, which it resembles, and the roots are dug late. Some I lifted today were more than sixteen inches long and sturdy. These I place in small deep boxes, a layer of earth, then a layer of roots, and as each box is filled I set it upright and cover the tops with a couple of inches of soil. These I take into the cold cellar, where the roots will presently start to grow and if kept dark and not too warm will produce the crisp bitter salad which around the holidays is so delicious. It takes about a month for the leaves to mature: but the process can be hastened or retarded by giving the boxes a little more or a little less warmth. It is necessary also to water the earth sparingly from time to time.

If only everyone could get his feet somewhere, somehow, down into the soil! Not farming necessarily, but at least a little plot of ground, a tree or two, bees, flowers—even a pot of tulips in the window! It is not in itself a panacea, it will not of itself make men happy or peaceful, but it will help, it will provide the soil wherein equanimity may germinate. It is a way toward reality: it links the soul of man with the creative spirit.

Genius is a kind of nakedness: genius is the honesty of an unusual mind.

NOVEMBER 5. We drove in the hills. The brilliant foliage of maples and ashes and most of the shrubs has disappeared, but the oaks are at their best—a best that is not to be excelled. With the sun upon them, especially the scrub oaks, or shining through them, there are no more brilliant or thrilling reds and scarlets and purples in all nature. I know well the burning bush of autumn! On distant hills, in grand spaces, the colors are subdued to deep rich bronzes shading down to brown, and where there is an intermingling of hemlocks, or pines, or spruces, the effect is a pageantry of color quite incomparable at any other time of the year—to me more satisfying in richness and variety of tone than the gaudier coloring of early autumn.

How it improves people for us when we begin to love them.

For many years I have been saving up references to the honeybee from the books I read. All literature from the beginning of time is sprinkled with more or less elaborate bee metaphors, often highly moral in their intent, but twisted and strained as to sober fact. For a thousand years nobody seemed to know that the "captain of the hive" was a queen and not a king. Hakluyt bases his exposition of the subject of colonization on the practices of the bee people.

"Wee reade that the Bees when they grow to be too many in their own hives at home, are wont to bee led out out by their Captaines to swarme abroad and seek themselves a new dwelling place. If the examples of the Grecians and Carthaginians of olde time and the practise of our age may not moove vs, yet let vs learne wisdome of these smal weake and vnreasonable creatures."

As to advice, be wary: if honest, it is also criticism.

NOVEMBER 6. It is unbelievable after such a day as yesterday to find the earth white this morning with a heavy fall of snow—the earliest in many years. We drove home in it— the brilliant colors of the hills bedimmed, dreary, dark; the little lakes, which yesterday were of brilliant greens and blues, today stone gray and cold. It looks like the dead of winter. Already the crows have begun flying, as they do in winter, with a kind of heavy weariness, across the barren fields.

Today in a garage I watched with positive delight a workman replace a worn tire: his extraordinary deftness. I have only two hands when three or four or more are so often necessary. He seemed to have at least four constantly at his disposal, for he used his foot and his knee, sometimes both feet and a knee, once or twice an elbow, as well as his arms and hands. It was truly a beautiful thing to see.

I chanced today upon verses called "Pale-Colored Caterpillars" which describe, gorgeously, a daily experience of my own at this time of year. They are by a writer, Winifred Welles, whom I am sorry I do not know:

"Now comes the fall when I am always meeting
*   ing*
* Pale-colored caterpillars in the grass,*

*Great, tight, green silk ones, pleating and
     unpleating,*
  *Smooth, creamy ones, a-wrinkle as they
     pass."*

Could there be a better description?

I read today in "Hyperion," Keats's defini-
tion of the "top of sovereignty":

> *"For to bear all naked ills,*
> *And to envisage circumstances all calm,*
> *. . This is the top of sovereignty."*

NOVEMBER 10. A belated summer day,
snatched from the clutches of old winter.

I worked with new lumber, sawing, fitting,
nailing—wholly absorbed and quite happy—
building another two-colony shelter for the
wintering of my bees. Some beekeepers I
know prefer to move all their colonies into a
basement room wherein the temperature can
be regulated, but I have found it far prefera-
ble to place each hive in a large stout box with
free entrance holes and plenty of shavings or
dry leaves packed around it to prevent sudden changes in temperature. It follows more
closely the immemorial and normal method
of the bees themselves, since they have sur-

vived through millions of years even in this climate with only the housing of hollow trees, or, more recently, the flimsy roofs of old barns or houses. By leaving them outside they utilize warm and sunny days throughout the winter for flying out with the dead bees or the refuse of the colony: keeping that perfect cleanliness which is the mark of the tribe. Under any system the prime requisite of good wintering is a plentiful supply of honey: for with food the bees themselves, by a constant motion of legs and wings, can easily raise the temperature of the hive by several degrees.

This year I have fed a number of the colonies that were deficient with thick sugar syrup, and every one of them seemed today, as I lifted them into the winter boxes, to be more than heavy enough with stores. It was such a still warm afternoon that the bees gave me no trouble at all. I shall have several more afternoons of work before completing the task, but it is both pleasant and interesting: I enjoy it.

Good people sometimes irritate us. Their well-proved virtues! We pay with grudging admiration for the approval they compel.

I do not think I shall find anything there that I have not here; nor anything then that I have not now.

Hurry is not the disease of the age, but the symptom of it. Men fear being quiet, facing themselves, and hurry to some new distraction.

When I went to France, there I was with myself, and the same in Pelham and Shutesbury. There are delightful things in Paris and in Cooleyville, but of themselves they are nothing to me if, being there, I do not know how to live greatly in my own spirit.

NOVEMBER 13. An Indian-summer day, still and warm and hazy, with a kind of golden balm in the air. Like an old man resting after labor.

One of the greatest, and most deceptive, passions now sweeping the world is the passion for security—safety. Nations demand it as though it were an inalienable right. Millions of men sacrifice to insure their lives and their property, demand old-age pensions, security against unemployment, ease during illness. All of these devices and mechanisms are well enough, if a man does not really put his trust in them: for there is, after all, no such thing as security in this world. No safety! The only resource for the soul of man is the cheerful acceptance of insecurity: steeling the spirit to bear whatever may happen. Nothing will take the place of inner fortitude. Here I stand: let anything happen!

"The delicate and gentle art of never getting there"—I practice so often with delight when I go to walk.

Today I reread one of those passages in Walt Whitman which strike up at one from the page like a flash of blinding light:
"To die is different from what anyone supposed—and luckier."

NOVEMBER 14. A vast flock of starlings whose maneuvers in the air I watched for some time, and with admiration. A squirrel, sitting up, eating snowberries; a small covey of pheasants darting under the hedge; a gray, low-toned day, full of feeling. I too live in the haze of autumn.

The sound of an axe in the hollow autumn wood—this I enjoy.

When the sense of adventure dies down, much of life that is good goes with it. Habit is a kind of death.

I have said it: let it go! If I had waited until I acquired the final truth, the ultimate beauty, I should never have said anything at all. I must go on—incomplete. It is the test of the writer—that he is sincere in his imperfections, honest in his limitations.

Commandment Number One of any truly civilized society is this: Let people be different.

We come to resemble that which we most admire.

NOVEMBER 16.

> I got up this morning,
> I put myself on
> Like a comfortable old coat.
> Holes in the elbows?
> I do not mind,
> I made them myself.

NOVEMBER 18. Pruning grapevines. All the leaves except the oak are down now, and in the morning the surface of the garden is hard and dry and cold. The bees are mostly in their winter quarters, safe and warm, the starlings are abroad, swift, wheeling flocks alighting in the meadows, the gray squirrels haunt the trees, though most of the acorns have fallen. I am silent and at peace.

Yesterday I was talking with an old country philosopher I know. He was laying a stone wall and commented on the indispensability of small stones to keep the large ones in place —make the wall solid.

"And I was thinkin'," said he, "of the need of small men, like me, to keep the big ones in place. They can't leave a man of us out."

"That's what they sometimes forget," said I.

"Yes, sir, they forget it—but it ain't fer long. Their wall falls down."

My friend is given to old-fashioned stories of the soil.

"They was once a time in New England when only a man with property could vote. Two brothers they was in Rhode Island, and one hadn't a nickel and couldn't vote. The other had a jackass and could. So they ast whether it was the man or the jackass that really voted."

He is convinced that almost all the troubles that plague the world are caused by the "almighty dollar."

"It's the dollar," says he, "that makes fools of every man jack of us. The more the dollars the bigger the fools—and *that's* the trouble with this here country of ours. Too many dollars in the hands of fools."

NOVEMBER 19. Working today with a quiet mind among my bees, finishing their bestowal in their winter boxes. The day has been fine and cool, all the world clad with sober gaiety in browns and tans and grays. All the leaves are down now, and the bareness is that of winter, yet the winter, upon a day like this of rich misty stillness, seems afar off. I dismiss every consideration of my daily task— all care banished—and go about these simple affairs of my garden. Surely there are few things that better "still the beating mind."

I tag myself with no tags: for when I accept another man's classification I accept also what that man means by the words he uses.

Do I believe in God? What God? What do you mean by God? Am I a socialist? What do *you* consider a socialist? A humanist? A farmer? A democrat?

NOVEMBER 20. Today we had a Visitor from the Unknown. About three o'clock, while I was at work pruning my apple trees and burning the brush in the chill air, I saw, far to the northward against the cold blue of the sky, a spot, a speck, that caught strongly the afternoon light of the sun. It seemed nearly over Deerfield and high above Mount Toby. A kite? It was far too high and as round as a bowl. A balloon? It had not that shape. I stood by my blazing brush fire looking up, marveling, with a strange thrill. It was clearly not an airplane: these we know well by now, in our valley.

It came majestically nearer, looking like a great silver fish swimming in the ocean of the air. The sunlight shone upon its burnished fins, and presently I saw the faint white glint of its breath caught outward in the frosty air. It seemed at first, at that great height and with nothing but the clouds and the sun to measure it by, that it was scarcely moving at all: and then I thought, with a sudden new perception of the wonder of the thing, that since it left Deerfield a moment ago and was now over Mount Warner it must be sailing through space at something like the speed of the swiftest railroad train—at least a mile a minute. It was inconceivable! All our road rushed out into the open air, craning its neck, shouting its comments, expressing its wonder. Now it was going straight into the declining sun: it had become a sunspot. And so with serene grandeur it passed over Northampton and down the Connecticut. Now it was a thousand feet, or more, above Mount Tom, and now a fading speck, in the sky, over Springfield.

What a thing is man!

It was the first great airship ever seen, I think, in our valley. It had flown in one day from its hangar in New Jersey to Boston and now homeward again across fields, mountains and rivers, to New York. A miracle: a visitor from the great unknown.

Where will men not fly, into what mysteries, through what wonders—if they do not falter, if they do not fear the unknown?

I was delighted, visiting the mountain weavers, to find this line from Marcus Aurelius on the door of their shop.

"Love the little trade thou hast learned and be content therewith."

Proverbs are half-truths, but the world, as Sancho Panza, that wise man, well knew, lives by half-truths. This, too, is a half-truth.

NOVEMBER 25. The rain was succeeded by a blustering storm from out of the north. I went out with my coat buttoned to the chin and lifted the last of the celery and brought it into the root cellar. Almost always, terrified by the blusterings of winter, I have been too early. The celery does better in the ground until the last moment before winter comes roaring down. Of course it is difficult to determine the *last moment*. I thought it was today. (December 10. I was quite right.)

You are in a hurry. Don't wait! I shall watch you go by. I shall stop here—oh, quietly. I shall think of you moving swiftly, victoriously. When you have hurried long enough, come back to me. I shall be here.

DECEMBER

IN THE COUNTRYMAN'S YEAR

---

*"I will make mention now of the works
of the Lord, and will declare the things that
I have seen."*

CHAPTER IX

DECEMBER IN THE COUNTRYMAN'S YEAR

DECEMBER 4. Admirable cool days for vigorous outdoor work. I mulched the strawberries and wheeled up many loads of humus from the compost heap of two years ago to cover the beds of crocuses, daffodils and tulips. One can live these days.

One bird stays with us most of the winter. An ardent, daring, encouraging bird, the blue jay. "Do it, do it," he cries, "do it, do it, do it."

Today I met a neighbor of mine whom I like to quiz, since he has the two requisites of the true philosopher: plenty of trouble—and humor. When I asked him how he was getting along, he responded with a broad smile:

"Even a blind pig can occasionally root up an acorn."

Life has rarely bored me: except momentarily, at tea parties.

DECEMBER 6. Sharp, cold weather. No snow as yet. Tony brought a load of wood, mostly white birch, and when I looked around for an axe with which to split some of the plump, round chunks, I found nothing but broken handles. I spent most of the afternoon at my bench working the old handle out of one of the heads and fitting in a new one. It is the kind of thing I delight heartily in doing. The new helve, bought of Mr Elder for fifty cents, was not the equal, in my eyes, of the helve I myself once long ago whittled out of a second-growth hickory stick, but it was well enough—good, smooth, white wood, and

I enjoyed putting it in. After that I tested it on a few of the birch chunks; it worked to perfection.

One of the joys of these wintry days is to step into the fruit cellar, where the apple crop is stored, and pick out a fine, red, ripe apple, a little waxy to the touch, but firm and juicy and sweet. To one who enjoys his nose as I do it is a perfect experience.

What! Did you really expect a revolution without yourself suffering anything? Did you? A comfortable, moderate revolution that would stop when you wanted it to stop, at the point where the world would be most agreeable for you to live in? So the Girondins, dreaming great dreams of a fairer France— until the tumbrils took them in. *More* liberty, *more* equality, *more* fraternity—so Danton and Robespierre, soon themselves to mount the guillotine. The circle completed, revolution having consumed itself, what remains for man but a return to his own soul? *There,* if he revolt, he may be sure of reform.

We are bored, not by living, but by not living enough.

DECEMBER 11. All night the snow fell silently, without a breath of wind; the first real snow of the year. This morning a world clad in spotless white. It is the beginning of the long daily darkness. The sun goes down near four o'clock, and the endless night does not break until seven in the morning. But what a time it is for turning inward: building a warm fire on the hearthstone of the spirit—and sitting there of long still evenings to consider great things that have gone by, and greater that are yet to come. A countryman's evening, and the joys of it—I could write an entire book to celebrate it!

I read today an article on Nova stars by a distinguished astronomer. Every fourth sentence was a confession of ignorance, and the whole mere speculation and supposition. The little we know, the best of us, compared with the illimitable! And yet there are those in this world who possess the only indispensable knowledge we call wisdom—how to live with themselves, this little life.

We are always expecting our friends to change: they are always repeating themselves.

The temptation to help directly by words, not indirectly by being what we are.

DECEMBER 13. A surprising fall: no really cold weather and the days crisp, sunny, delightful. All the countryside is full of the sounds and sights of thrifty farm activities which the mild weather so gloriously invites. If a farmer or gardener can go into the winter with his "fall work" well out of the way he feels comfortable indeed. Yesterday I saw my neighbors drawing out the last of their onions in great, prosperous loads, or spreading black manure from smoking piles upon the open land; and in one field, just below North Amherst, they were actually plowing with two teams, around and around. All the swamps and wells are full of water—we have had good rains recently—removing one of the farmer's familiar worries. Here and there one can hear, resounding through the crisp air, the hollow music of axes in new timber where the farmer is cutting his winter supply of wood.

I worked last night on the hillside until after the dark had fallen, leaving only a dim afterglow in the west reflected in the ponds and pools of the valley, glowing like eyes that see best in the dark. I saw the lights of Whately and Plainfield prick out one by one like little holes in the hills, and on the Hadley road, traveling lights, lifting, shifting, blinking out and coming suddenly alive again— cars making their way homeward from the town. I like it all.

So many men I know are feverishly seeking to make over the "system," who have themselves never learned how to live. If they could tomorrow reconstruct social institutions they would be no happier, no braver, no nobler than they are today, and would soon be agitating and organizing to bring about still newer reconstructions. I am certain that one Utopian I know would be desperately unhappy in his Utopia, if he had it.

I heard a man today complaining of the trouble he has with his property—but he could so easily have less of it!

"The hay appeareth, and the tender grass showeth itself, and herbs of the mountain are gathered"—the Book was made for those who live on the land. "The lambs are for thy clothing and the goats are the price of the field."

Readings of my youth!—how well I remember them—common things richly glorified—"every pot in Jerusalem . . . holiness unto the Lord of hosts."

I can hear still the voice of the Scotch preacher, and the words he read, that shook me in my central parts. The psalms he gloried in, and the marching verses of the prophets; rich passages from Isaiah, full of poetry, deep with thought; the drama of Job and his comforters; and stark tales of the Kings, good and bad, and both gathered soon unto their fathers.

How much indeed I owe that old Book, how much the stern old man who read from it, and did not know of the devotion of one little boy sitting there below him in the hard wooden seat.

DECEMBER 14. I have had my second-best blue suit cleaned and pressed by Walsh the tailor. I have tried on my old hat and examined my overcoat to see if it will last another winter. I am prepared for the revolution which I am told will soon be upon us.

When I am in the city I am afraid for America.

DECEMBER 16. Today, arising late, I saw that the world was gloomy, with lowering clouds, and soggy snow, and a dull wind blowing; and I thought that I would find some pessimistic friend and talk with him for a long time, despondently and sorrowfully. I should come home afterwards feeling much happier.

I read today a passage in a book I have enjoyed for many years, *The Private Papers of Henry Ryecroft,* which expresses better than I could do it a thought I have often had:

"And one may safely say that, of all the ages since a coin first became the symbol of power, ours is that in which it yields to the majority of its possessors the poorest return in heart's contentment."

It is idle to consider whether what you have to give, whether you yourself, are of any use or importance to the world. Be it, give it; it is all you have. No one was ever yet able to fix his own price: this is determined, like that of any other commodity, by the demand. Some people will want what you have or what you are, and some will not. It is a market that can sometimes be rigged temporarily: never for long.

DECEMBER 18. What a morning! Ten degrees below zero. Sunshine, pale blue sky, a few fleecy clouds. We have four or five inches of snow on the ground: not a breath of air stirring: the smoke of breakfast fires rising straight upward from the chimneys. All the hemlocks and spruces carry tremendous loads of snow which a single breath of air will dislodge.

In my old coat, old rough leggings, warm old gloves, I tramped in the spotless world. Not any track of adventurer or explorer ahead of me! But there was a rabbit.

I heard sleigh bells, strange sound in a time of motorcars. In one house, as I passed, a child playing "The Londonderry Air"—I came presently from the vast wilderness of the snow to a path and thus to a trampled lane where cattle had been driven up, and then to the great bare road.

With untold riches on every hand to be had for the taking, it is sad to see men contenting themselves with trash.

So often, especially in reading of the swift competence of the great, I am cast down by the thought of my own want of talent. At such times it comforts me to repeat that sonnet of Shakespeare which begins:

"When in disgrace with fortune and men's eyes
I all alone beweep my outcast state."

If Shakespeare could "envy this man's art, that man's scope"—why——!

And today, reading Sir William Rothenstein's memoirs, I came across this dramatic glimpse of Whistler—of all men—doubting his own work:

"Climbing the stairs we found the studio in darkness. Whistler lighted a single candle. He had been gay enough during dinner, but now he became very quiet and intent, as though he forgot me. Turning a canvas that faced the wall, he examined it carefully up and down, with the candle held near it, and then did the like with some others, peering closely into each. There was something tragic, almost frightening, as I stood and waited, watching Whistler; he suddenly looked old, as he held the candle with trembling hands, and stared at his work, while our shapes threw restless, fantastic shadows all around us. As I followed him silently down the stairs, I realized that even Whistler must often have felt his heart heavy with the sense of failure. A letter to Fantin-Latour, published long after, in which he regretted that, while a student, he had not learned to draw like Ingres, reminded me vividly of what I had seen that night."

DECEMBER 19. A windy dawn: cold blue light on the snow: faint streaks of pink above the gaunt bare trees in the east. The limbs of the dark hemlocks heave and sway, and there is no sign of human life anywhere upon the hill or in the wide and windy valley. A cold dawn: an empty world.

Inbred poetry: so much now written by poets for poets—or critics: there is too little that moves the souls of men generally. "The poets," says A.E., "have dropped out of the divine procession and sing a solitary song. They inspire nobody to be great."

Reading today from Sidney Lanier's *Poem Outlines,* I ran across this sentence:

"A man does not reach any stature of manhood until, like Moses, he kills an Egyptian . . . and flies into the desert of his own soul."

How well I remember killing my Egyptian!

DECEMBER 20. Today, while meditating on the eternal verities, I was called, urgently, to carry a stepladder downstairs.

I have made friends with one of the most intelligent, sensitive, affectionate dogs that ever I met in my life. She belongs to a neighboring family and is part German sheep dog, large and active, with extraordinarily bright and expressive eyes. Her name is Djinn. We had quite a time getting acquainted, since she is shy and has to be wooed. She loves to have sticks thrown in air, which she is clever at catching in her mouth. Once or twice a day she comes over and leaves her calling card— a bit of wood or bark—on our steps to let me know that she is anxious to see me. I can hardly go out anywhere that she does not spy me and come bounding across the road with her ears up and eyes gleaming. This morning, as I started on my walk, I heard something stirring behind me. I turned and there was Djinn, looking as humble as you please, tail down, head quite abject, eyes faltering. She knew perfectly well that she had no business to follow me. She has strict orders not to leave home. I looked at her sternly.

"Djinn," said I, "you ought to be ashamed of yourself!"

Her eyes said plainly that she was; but there was the faintest propitiatory stirring of her tail. She came crawling hopefully a step or two forward. I could not resist it.

"Well," said I, "I haven't time to take you back. Come on along; we'll walk together."

She understood perfectly. The transformation was instantaneous. Up went her head and tail, and there was a brilliant, half-roguish gleam in her eye. She ran by me, just brushing my legs to let me know how happy she was—she does not welcome petting—and sprang out ahead of me. How she enjoyed it! I wish I had as much delight from my nose as she does from hers—eagerly tracing rabbit trails, surprising squirrels by dodging more quickly around the oak trees than they. She

likes to stop and listen just as I do. She lifts
one foot, stretches a little forward, tilts her
head, and devotes all her senses to catching
the rustle of a partridge in the dry leaves or
the chattering of a chipmunk in a stone wall.

And yet how courteous and sensitive she is
not to forget that she is walking with me.
When in her eagerness she has galloped too
far ahead, she waits for me to come up, glancing back at me with mouth open in a wide
smile and a look of perfect affection and enjoyment in her eyes, as though she said:

"Master, I love you. I am glad to be with
you on such a fine morning. I enjoy everything I see."

She came back with me a little tired, trot-
ting comfortably at my side—for she had run
at least ten times as far as I had walked—
and as soon as we got home found a comfortable spot on the sunny porch where she
could lie down to rest.

DECEMBER 21. At the Farmers' Club today
Whitmore was talking of the foreigners who
have come to our valley, in contrast with the
native-born.

"At least," said he, "the foreigners observed

the conventions. They came here with their trousers on: the native-born came with them off."

To avoid thought, a friend of mine takes his dog along when he goes for a walk—to interrupt him.

Life is too brief. I had a friend whom I intended always to know better, enjoy more deeply. Yesterday he died.

DECEMBER 23. To Shutesbury hill for Christmas greens. Silent wintry woods, full of snow. The last pink sky of an early sunset with the exquisite tracery of bare trees against it. Lights coming on in evening windows, cattle bawling, dark figures in snow-filled roads, going home. The spell of New England winter days.

Today I went into Elder's hardware store and found them selling nails, screws, axes, also kitchen stoves and washing machines, also sewer pipe and pumps, to the strains of Verdi's *Traviata*. Wonderful the age of the radio!

I will live now, I will enjoy now: yesterday is past, and I am not sure of tomorrow.

The old world we knew has gone—utterly gone—and we have not yet entered upon the new. The World War was the dividing line. Where is the tremendous upheaval of the human spirit which will bring order out of this chaos? I see men of force: but where are the prophets, the poets, the true leaders? I see men tearing down the ruins: where are the builders?

DECEMBER 25. Christmas Day. Fierce cold, yet dry and clear, the snowy earth radiant with sunshine, such a day as only the north can know. The newspapers say that all records for low temperature for this time of year have been broken, but our gaiety has in no wise been dimmed. We have skated—all hands—on the pond, we have coasted on the hill, we have tramped the wintry roads—and come in glowing, to shake ourselves out of coats and mufflers and seek the roaring open fires. At noon what a turkey, and everything that goes with it—what pumpkin pies! The long table quite full, a tree that touched the ceiling, cries of astonishment and joy from all the little boys and girls, and many surprises and much laughter—and music in the house—and dancing. It has been a good Christmas Day.

DECEMBER 28. This morning, walking in my snow-covered garden, I forgot myself into enjoyment.

Few people know how beautiful a garden can be in winter—the sun glistening on the snow—blue shadows north of the pines—orchard trees like lace against the steely sky. This morning I stood long near my covered hives, each of which wore a hood of snow, to watch the bees flying out, lifting in the clear air, returning swiftly to the warmth of the hive.

I discovered today, in the Book of Proverbs, a command that I, as a beekeeper, fully support and commend, demanding that the populace generally obey it:

"Eat thou honey because it is good."

Reading Sir James Jeans's explanation of the universe which, a thousand years from now, will probably appear as ridiculous as the reasons soberly given by Herodotus for the inundations of the Nile.

I know! It is not limitation of life that plagues us. Life is not limited: it is the limitation of our *awareness* of life.

One foot in a garden—at least that, for joy.

JANUARY

IN THE COUNTRYMAN'S YEAR

"If a man does not keep pace with his companions, perhaps it is because he hears a different drummer."—H. D. THOREAU.

CHAPTER X

JANUARY IN THE COUNTRYMAN'S YEAR

JANUARY 6. The snow: the first of any consequence in several weeks—serious, businesslike snow, fine-grained, slanting downward upon gray meadows, brown furrows. The air is perfectly still, the heavens hang low. Each branch of the hemlock carries steadily its heaping loads, the roofs begin to be stoutly thatched with it. I hear the call of a crow, lonesome and muffled in the heavy air. We are shut in by the snow: no tracks, no trails, no roads to the outward world. All is smooth and white and clean.

A bright fire burns upon my hearth, I turn with a sigh of comfort to my busy desk.

Today there called at my door a man with glowing eyes, an ardent voice, an eager way of shaking hands—every characteristic of one on fire for saving the human race. Was he a great religious leader? Prophet? Poet? No, he was selling silver polish.

This morning I put a gnarly white-pine chunk, chopped here on my own land, upon the fire: and the odor of it burning brought such a wave of homesickness for the north woods—and the open land—as I cannot describe. The odor of campfires!

There has just come in the mail the most gorgeous seed catalogue that ever I saw in my life: from Sutton in England. We spent half the evening gobbling it up: onions six inches across, beans eighteen inches long! We will plant this year seed from the old sod.

JANUARY 10. The best of these fine winter days, when the garden is full of snow, is my morning tramp in my old warm coat, with my stick in my hand. The inner glow, the lift of the mind, as I tread the new snow with the sun coming up over the distant village! Life is good. I ask, indeed, why I am here, what it is all about, and have no answer, and yet how beautiful the wintry trees, how heady the morning air!

The nugget oneself delves from the hard ore of an old book is worth many plums picked from another man's literary pudding.

We like people who enjoy life. "Mirth" is one of the commonest words in Pepys' diary: we like Pepys better than Boswell, or Johnson either, because he is healthier. It is the unending charm of that old reprobate, John Falstaff. The pale, the faded, the sad are soon rubbed off the printed page: the man of gusto etches himself upon our hearts.

Never blame a man for qualities he does not possess: as that he is blind in one eye, or that he lacks tact, or knowledge; judge him by the use he makes of qualities he does possess.

SUNDAY. A quiet, dull winter day. Much reading: friends came in to talk: a call or so: a little good music: a short walk to look at the tranquil earth.

Blessed that man who has a citadel in his own soul: a place where, having fought, he may retire for peace.

Sorrow is often the price we pay for love: it is worth it.

This idea, this vision, this bit of life, seems interesting to me, somehow beautiful. I will put it in my Book. Why not? What else have I?

Consider, after losses of goods or money— am I not the same man I was yesterday? Have I not the same friends, the same passion of interest, as for nature, or books, or music?

Have I not still my thoughts, my occupation?
Have I not my dear family?

Few men ever have all the suffering they
can bear: many think they have.

JANUARY 14. It has been an extraordinarily
mild winter thus far. A warm rain the other
day swept the country bare of snow. It is like
late March: I was told that a farmer on
Mount Toby had tapped two maple trees and
got sap enough to make a saucer of syrup.
This is what the old New Englander calls
the "January thaw."

I was out this afternoon pruning the grapes
—a task I have never yet trusted to any
other hands than my own; looking after the
apples in the fruit cellar; bringing in more
chicory roots and a barrel of rhubarb, for
forcing. We have just eaten the last of our
celery crop. The winter apples are at their
best, the Baldwins particularly.

One of the things that irritates me extremely
—in short, makes me angry—is the insulting
disregard, common in this country, of natural
beauty. Piles of old tin cans and rubbish
dumped in a beautiful roadside brook—I

know of such a case—motorcars left to rust in open meadows—fine trees needlessly hacked to make way for eyesore telephone poles—all billboards whatsoever!—these things are evidences of our lack of civilization.

Not long ago I ran across an excellent addition to the litany, proposed by the Council for the Preservation of Rural England (1930) which ought also to be adopted in this country:

"From all destroyers of natural beauty in this parish and everywhere: from all polluters of earth, air and water: from all makers of visible abominations: from jerry-builders, disfiguring advertisements, road hogs, and spreaders of litter: from the villainies of the rapacious and the incompetencies of the stupid: from the carelessness of individuals and the somnolence of Local Authorities: from all foul smells, noises, and sights—good Lord, deliver us!"

Observation without sympathy never leads to comprehension—oftener to apprehension.

Tenderness of understanding is often wanting in men of intellectual power. They are

without pity, and without pity the world is
iron and frost.

I could sit here this wintry morning and
write a poem—or an essay—possibly a book!
—on the joy of an open fire, such as I have
burning here upon my hearth. It is the soul
of the house: the center of its joy, the inspira-
tion of its labor. And yet why write any such
poem or essay, when writers from the beginning have expended their genius upon it? I
have found many a passage well worth pre-
serving in my own reading. Here is one from
a scandalous old blackguard who lived during
the Italian renaissance—I mean Aretino—
who could not, after all, knowing such enjoy-
ments as these, have been wholly black:

"Four dry logs have in them all the cir-
cumstance necessary to a conversation of four
or five hours, with chestnuts on the plate and
a jug of wine between the legs. Yes, let us
love winter, for it is the spring of genius."

And De Quincey, the opium eater, had this
to say:

"Surely everyone is aware of the divine
pleasures which attend a winter fireside:
candles at four o'clock, warm hearthrug, tea,

a fair tea-maker, shutters closed, curtains flowing in ample draperies on the floor, whilst the wind and rain are whistling audibly without. . . . I am not 'particular,' as people say, whether it be snow, or black frost, or wind so strong that (as Mr —— says) 'you may lean your back against it like a post.' "

JANUARY 17. Another heavy warm rain last night: this morning mild and clear, with the meadow brook overrunning its banks. Such weather will "shorten the time until the first of April," as our farmers say.

Enormous flocks of English starlings are about. They visit the barn and henyards and even fly into the henhouses. The bees were out in swarms to enjoy the mild weather. I have been at work pruning my peach trees.

When we have a "spell of weather" like this the newspapers break out with appropriate items: "Wild Geese Fly Northward." "Bay State Man Mows Lawn." "Mrs Dyer Finds Blossoms in Her Garden."

I met old Mr L——, who says the weather "acts mighty funny," but he can always remember some winter, back in '84 or '93, to beat it.

"You'd predict some snug weather yet, wouldn't you, Mr L——?" I remarked.

"Well, I ain't no prophet nor yet the son of a prophet, but I'd bet something—if I was a bettin' man—on there bein' a good spell o' winter yet—a dang good spell. I'd bet on it—if I was what you'd call a bettin' man."

Boswell, said Johnson, had a "gust" for London, for the city: my gust is for the country: quiet days I love best and simple things.

The new magic words now sweeping the world are "control," "management." We are taking, or trying to take, vast new domains of human life out of the realm of accident and chance. Birth is to be controlled, money managed, industry planned, production regulated. I sat today for a long time listening: I heard no one say anything about self-control.

Preferring not to write about what I do not or cannot know, I do not write much about God.

I have enjoyed attending several farmers' meetings this winter and hearing those sturdy, hardheaded, common-sense men talk of their problems. I think it takes more of a man, more brains, more character, more courage, more bodily vigor, to be a truly successful farmer than it requires in any other calling I know. A farmer must know much of many things, not only the multitudinous details of his own ancient calling, but he must be a ready carpenter, mechanic, blacksmith, painter, stone mason; he must know how to use cement or tinker a motorcar; he must have enough chemical knowledge to mix and apply fertilizers; he must understand animals and animal diseases: and above all, in these roaring days of the trader, he must be able to buy and sell shrewdly. Most of the farmers I know fail because they are not good business men.

Look twice—doubt again.

Leonardo da Vinci, thinking of death, how reasonable it was, how inevitable, the "will of the Prime Mover"—yet "in the depth of his heart something waxed indignant, could not and would not submit to reason."

How well I know that unreasonableness —and that indignation!

JANUARY 22. New England is vindicated at last. This morning, after a day of bitter and cutting wind, the thermometer is at zero. Everything frozen up, including some of our pipes: and yet the sun rises with rare beauty, and all the world is clear and still. The frosty air stings one's face, prickles in one's nose, sets all the blood to racing warmly. The snow creaks and snaps under one's feet, and the sunshine on the silvery fields is blinding to the eyes.

One of the sports of our neighborhood is to fight thermometers. We challenge our neighbors: we were 10 degrees below, only to find that they were 12 degrees, and East Street appears with 15 degrees to beat both of us.

This I know well: that the chief part of every life consists of small things. If we have not learned how to live with them and enjoy them, we have not learned to live. It is strange how competently, even nobly, many men will ride out the great storms of sorrow and tragedy, who are wrecked upon the little reefs that litter the calm waters of their daily lives.

Blessed is the man who can enjoy the small

things, the common beauties: the little day-by-day events, sunshine on the fields, birds on the bough, breakfast, dinner, supper: the daily paper on the porch, a friend passing by. So many people who go afield for enjoyment leave it behind them at home.

JANUARY 23. I had a man in today to fix my motor. I stood watching him with admiration: the skill of him, the easy, swift effectiveness. His knowledge! What a necessary, indispensable person, this man in his greasy coat, with his black hands. How he was restoring my powers, saving my time, serving my comfort! It came to me suddenly to ask myself, as I stood there, whether I was of any use to him. Did I likewise add to his comfort or increase his powers? Was I also indispensable to him? Did he consider me at all, save as the source of a few necessary dollars which he might as easily make from anyone else as from me? And what had dollars, anyway, to do with the human relationships between us?

If the artist, the poet, the prophet, does not exchange services with the mechanic, the plowman, the wood sawyer, of what use is

he to the state? If the artist merely creates
for other artists, how is the world illuminated? Why do artists and writers gather in
such curious defensive groups, feeding upon
one another's approval, growing anaemic, ef-
fecting nothing? I should like to exchange
benefits with my greasy-garmented mechanic.
I should like to be as useful to him—so that
he knew it—as he is to me, as I know it.

"He who reigns within himself," says Milton, "is more than a king. . . . Real and sub-
stantial liberty is rather from within than
from without."

What difference does it make what people
think? You are not required to live their lives,
but your own.

I have a friend here who delights in what
I call "property dreaming." He is a large,
slow man, with a dull eye. He has little money
or little hope of any and no one to leave it to
if he had, but he delights in going out on a
bit of bare New England hillside which he
owns and sitting down under a pine tree and

dreaming of the house he would like to build there—but never will. He has planned it out to the last detail. He knows where the living-room register is to be placed, how the taps in the kitchen are to be turned on. He has planted a lilac at the doorway and trained a Virginia creeper over the porch. His books he has arranged in a little cubby which he has set aside as a study—there is a miniature fireplace in the corner—so that he can turn from his easy chair and take down, at arm's length, his favorite copy of *David Copperfield*. This he dreams, although he never had in his life, or needed, a study, and never reads a book. It is the *David Copperfield* of his boyhood, the beautiful, romantic, vague, faraway *David Copperfield* he has placed in the tiny shelf at his elbow. There is a breakfast nook wherein to serve the apples which he picks from his own tree and a vase for the roses which he intends to grow. So he sits there in the rocky soil under his barren pine tree and dreams his property dreams. I think it gives him no end of pleasure. It stays his age and enriches his declining years.

It is a kind of property dreaming I do not know.

At a town meeting last night I heard again a story that has become traditional in New England. We delight in it, because it exhibits us in such a triumphant light compared with the boastful West. A breezy stranger blows into our hills and comments slightingly upon our miniature farms, the stones in our fields, and what he calls our "poor improvements."

"I don't see," he remarks finally, "how you folks get a living up here."

"Where ye from, stranger?" queries as farmery a looking old farmer as there is in the valley.

"I'm from Kansas. We've got farms out there as big as this whole town. In Kansas we waste more than enough to feed the entire state of Vermont."

"I ain't a doubt of it," our old farmer responds dryly. "I ain't a doubt ye waste too much. I got mortgages on six or eight o' your big farms out there that ain't bein' paid. I reckon I'll have to take holt o' three or four of 'em myself."

The joke of it is that this story could easily be true. I knew, some years ago, just such a farmery old farmer who loaned thousands of dollars on Western farms—and lost it.

JANUARY 30. There is no time like this—such quiet wintry days, here in the country—for friendship and for the enjoyment of the richest savings of our common life—I mean books and music. Last night we attended a remarkably fine concert, and I had great joy out of a rendering of Beethoven's second symphony. I can understand faintly, I think, how a Shakespeare tragedy could be written, and even a Parthenon built, but a Beethoven symphony is a burst of the creative spirit that is, to me, beyond conception how it could be done. So completely to enter into a man's soul, and comfort it, and satisfy it, and wholly make it happy! How did he know when and where to put in the little curly sweetnesses of the flutes to ravish the senses, when the great pom-pom of the bass viols, and how, everything being quiet, could he think of such exquisite things for the first violin to say? And oh, the cellos, like deep water running through autumn trees: and the harps, heavenly in their resonances! Is there any greater creation of the human spirit? When everything else goes, one can still be happy—if he can have music.

A critic I met today argued that this particular small-town orchestra ought not to attempt the great and difficult symphonies: let it give us more or less popular music like the Grainger orchestrations of old English ballads and folk dances. I did not agree at all. What is an orchestra for if not to play symphonies? If not to give us, a musically starved people, some access to the greatest expressions in this field of the human spirit? What if it is not as technically perfect as my friend would have it?

And why expect the musicians to do everything? Have we not, as listeners, to contribute something out of the music of our own souls? The profit in enjoyment that comes to us from any concert, as from any book or play, depends exactly upon what we ourselves bring to it. Nature itself yields us little joy save as we observe it with a seeing eye, a hearing ear, an understanding spirit. I can pick flaws in plenty with the technique of the landscape I see across my own valley, yet I enjoy it keenly.

There is something about great music, something within it—as there is about the Berkshire Hills, or a great play like *King Lear*—that cannot be wholly spoiled. Something great inevitably gets through!

FEBRUARY

IN THE COUNTRYMAN'S YEAR

*"Study to be quiet, and to do your own
business, and to work with your own hands."*

CHAPTER XI

FEBRUARY IN THE COUNTRYMAN'S YEAR

FEBRUARY 4. Authentic winter! January weakens its vigor with its proverbial "thaw," and March has yielding days of springlike weather, but February, with us, is the best that the northern winter can do: stern, unrelenting, unforgiving! "Tight cold," my neighbor calls it—and yet, to one who loves it, what could be finer? Mornings like these which register 15 or 20 degrees Fahrenheit, but clear, chaste, sunny, with sparkle and life in the air. The snow is not deep but packed hard even in the woods. I took a long tramp yesterday, walking across the crusty fields to the new forestry plantings. The virgin earth was like a map, with tracings of rabbit runs, the footprints of mice and of partridges, and here and there a galloping dog or perhaps a fox, and once the proof that a squirrel had ventured out into the snowy world. I found many little holes dug through the snow to the leaves and the berries and the roots underneath. The tag alder, this time of year, shaken by the wind, scatters from its small brown cones a shower of seeds upon the snow—manna for wild, shy birds and mice and squirrels.

I find that these secluded winter days promote my work—the quiet, long forenoons, the still evenings.

Charge any common thing with a high voltage of understanding and emotion and you have the materials for a work of art.

It is the spirit of adventure, not the mechanism of it, that matters. Ulysses went to sea in a rowboat, Lindbergh in an airplane.

Again this day I have been thinking how little thankful I am for being here: for the joy I have in seeing, hearing, smelling, feeling, knowing. I might not have been alive at all. A billion chances—and I am here! I sit at the table of the gods and quaff the nectar of life. Wonder of wonders: I am not only here, but know that I am here.

FEBRUARY 5. My years fall away on a day like this. On a day like this I take a part of my immortality. We had yesterday a roaring hullabaloo of a storm, with wild gusts of northern wind driving the fine snow across the countryside, choking up the roads, piling drifts beyond the fences, tufting the roofs and the sheltered trees. Altogether a blizzard, the first of the winter. I struggled through it to the deserted town—one must have food even on such a day—and positively enjoyed the experience.

But this morning! I was out at sunrise. The fury of the storm had spent itself, and all the world lay white and still. A few fleecy pink clouds floated high in the heavens, and every tree cast a rich blue shadow. The air was sharp and frosty—infinitely exhilarating. The fields, the orchard, the roads were full of drifted billows, marked by wind riffles, like beach sand. It was so still that the smoke of breakfast fires rose straight to the sky, where they were plumed in pink and silver, exquisitely iridescent with the rays of the rising sun.

I had to dig out the bee boxes which were entirely covered by the drifts, else the patient population of the hives might have been smothered. Before I had gone far with this exhilarating labor I found the perspiration dripping from under my cap even though my ears and fingers were nipping cold. How good the pull of the muscles, how sharp and sweet and clear the morning air! With each cascade of snow, I threw up a spray of pearls and diamonds.

If one could imagine himself living *inside* of a diamond and that diamond full of sunlight—radiated and reflected from every facet, sparkling upon every point until the glory was bewildering—it would give a poor idea of what this morning has been like.

I stop in the midst of my intense labor to sharpen my pencils. I sit up to the open fire

and with my knife slowly and neatly sharpen
my pencils, brushing the shavings from the
hearth into the fire. My mind goes free for a
moment. I rest. I think of my snow-clogged
garden and of my bees safe in their winter
boxes. I recall a treasured line from one of the
essays of Montaigne. I wish spring would
come. I think of going fishing with my friend
Waugh and quite unexpectedly recall the passage in Izaak Walton on "grave men" which
years ago I committed with delight to memory:

"Grave men of sour complexion, money-
getting men, these poor-rich men that we
Anglers pity and stand in no need to borrow
their thoughts to imagine ourselves happy."

I think of several other curious matters, not
one of them duties, growing more cheerful
every moment, and presently I go back to
my laborious desk with a refreshed spirit. It
is well to break up one's intensity. The old
candlelight writers and fire menders had the
better of us: they were forced to stop from
time to time to snuff their candles or poke the
fire. And so charm crept into their lives and
their work.

FEBRUARY 8. It being a mild day, I went out into the garden with hammer and staples to mend the grape arbors. It is little enough of outdoor work the gardener can do at this time of year. The snow was deep and soft. Thereafter I examined some of the young apple trees for fruit spurs and the peach trees for borers. The bees were out by thousands: a people given to the best of habits. This winter an extraordinary number of crows have wintered near us in the marshes, and hunger has made them so bold that they come in close around the compost heaps and hen-yard. I have enjoyed watching them. Today I examined their tracks in the snow: not clean-cut, but dabbled with the marks of wing and tail feathers. One old crow—there seems to be but one that does it—sets the four front toes of each foot down like a mitten, three together and one separate: I suppose that crows are as different as human beings, if one could come to know them.

I have already planned, in my mind, what I shall do next spring with every foot of land I have to till.

Hopeless!—the man who moves only when he is afraid.

We are all, tooth and nail, seeking what we consider best in this world: where we differ is in our conception of what is best.

A spice of wickedness preserves many a book—*old* wickedness, which has lost its sting but retains its humor.

FEBRUARY 11. We are now taking the profits of our extended garden: not merely the stored apples and potatoes and carrots and beets (the latter packed in moss), but actual fresh growing things. Too few gardeners seem to know of such possibilities or to risk the slight trouble connected with them. We have now every day the most delicious of all salads: witloof chicory, which I brought into the basement from the cold root cellar a month ago. A delicious, crisp bitterness, as fine as any I ever tasted. Cut back, it continues to come up so that one can have several crops from the same box. I shall raise more of it next summer, planting a little earlier to get larger roots. We are also having an abundance of rhubarb for sauce or pies. In November I took up several of the largest roots in the garden—which ought anyway to be thinned out—and placed each in a barrel, packing it around and covering it lightly with sand. I left it out to freeze hard—it has to be convinced that it has gone through the winter!—and then brought it into the basement. Watered slightly and kept dark, it will produce within a few weeks a tremendous crop of the tenderest, pinkest, mildest stalks imaginable—much better in quality, we think, than that produced in the spring garden.

An ill world and an evil, one sometimes thinks, looking at it superficially—the day-by-day cruelty, cheapness, corruption shown in the disquieting columns of the press—but one idea, one great and beautiful curative idea, I think I have seen growing through the years. I heard it expressed long ago by the Negro leader, Booker T. Washington:

"You cannot keep the Negro in the gutter without staying there with him."

I have seen it clear in Henry Ford's repeated admonition that the prosperity of industry rests, not upon the exploitation of labor, but upon making labor itself prosperous —thus enabling the workman to buy the products of industry.

Science, above all, is shot through with it: for how leave plague spots of tuberculosis, or typhus, or hookworm in any part of the world without endangering our own children?

I felt the growth of the idea when the League of Nations was organized, wherein the world agreed that one nation cannot exploit or bully another without involving and injuring all people, everywhere, upon this planet.

If this idea, that men are inextricably bound together, that the welfare of each is the welfare of all—if only this idea can continue to grow, to become greater and stronger, many human ills will disappear.

I would not have thought it possible, but my friend Dyer has written an entire book on the great American rocking chair. It has a lure and a lore of its own.

FEBRUARY 21. A great golden day of solitude! The morning came with surpassing loveliness;

it was frosty and still, with white fields and trees set in a mystery of soft blue haze through which, at last, in waves of rosy light, came the morning sun.

I built a roaring fire of birch logs upon my hearth, and with books to the right of me and books to the left of me—and plenty of white paper to write upon—I charged like the Light Brigade. Such a day for absorbing labor!

In the late afternoon I walked up to the village—lest we starve!—with my head full of days gone by, events half forgotten—and came back with packages under both arms, walking between the huge snow piles which guard all our walks and roads.

"Here I am," said I to myself, "a complete man—with nothing left to be desired. In my right hand I have chops, a loaf of bread, a wedge of cheese, a pat of butter. So shall the animal be quieted. In my left I have the old world and the new—the past, the present and (if I am sharp enough) the future! For I am bringing home not only the morning newspaper but Church's life of Lord Bacon—for both of which I have an eager appetite. I have only to open the book, put in my nose, and I am magically transported three hundred years

into the past and can mingle with the greatest
spirits of one of the greatest moments of all
human experience. I can know Bacon and
Shakespeare, Essex, Coke, and the great
Elizabeth herself far more completely than
ever they were known in their own time or to
one another—I can know them better than
my own famous contemporaries, Roosevelt,
or Wilson, or Edison, or Henry Ford, for I
can know what they were doing secretly, what
letters they were writing, how they tricked
and lied and intrigued, how they loved and
struggled and failed, what brave dreams they
dreamed. I can know all this as well as I
know their public acts and experiences. So
it is that I have with me, under my arm, a
great past.

I have also a great present—if only I can
understand it. I have the day's copy of the
Springfield *Republican,* fresh from that
blessed emporium where the floor is worn
through with much passing—Hastings' news
store. Here in an hour I can survey the doings
of the world from Paris to Peru, from Washington to Amherst—of such a world as no one
ever saw before, touched, I think, with in-
sanity, or perhaps intoxicated with some

brand of heady liquor not known even to the most sophisticated of cup-lovers.

What a rich man am I! Enough this day for the body, and enough and more for the mind and the spirit. A fire glowing on the hearth, and if I would glance out through the window, a world of surpassing beauty: New England winter with the sun upon it!

A wonderful moment I find chronicled in a book I am reading: Leonardo da Vinci commenting upon the letter of Christopher Columbus (April 29, 1493) "anent the recently discovered India Isles above Ganges."

"How little he knows!" observes Leonardo sadly—this according to Merezhkowski. "And how much he accomplished! But I, with all my knowledge, am at a standstill. . . . Do not my eyes see farther than the eyes of Columbo, the blind prophet . . . or is such the lot of man: that one must be a seer in order to know, and blind in order to do?"

FEBRUARY 22. In the afternoon I tramped to Mill Valley to see the ice cutters at work, but the pond was open water and the cutting at an end. So I stopped at the mill, sniffing

at the doorway, looking in with pleasure at
the great fat bags of grain, the ancient noisy
machinery, the rafters gray with the undis-
turbed dust of half a century. I walked on up
the road, meeting many wood sleds, full-
loaded, on their way to town, the brass bells
hung from the horses' collars jangling in the
still air. A jolly driver waved his mittened
hand at me as he passed. Even the slightest
intimation of spring, as today, with warm
sunshine and gushing rivulets in every rut,
brings the farmers to long-neglected tasks.
I saw a man on a tall ladder striking the ice
from the overloaded eaves of his house. I saw
in the woods the flash of a lifted axe before I
heard the sound of it. A vast flock of starlings
cried in a bare elm top; there were hens
scratching and cackling in sunny barn doorways; and cattle, long mewed up in dusky
stables, yawned complacently in the open
yards or scratched their rumpled hides upon
convenient posts. I saw a crew of stout work-
men with shovels on their shoulders, come to
dig out the side drains and let off the melting
snow. I met the parson, and we stood for
some time in the broad road, with the open

sky above, and a touch of spring in the air, discussing the fate of the nation.

When nations do wrong and leadership is weak and congresses futile, I know that in far country places the unobserved world goes onward with its daily affairs, winter wears to its end, spring comes on, life turns with serenity upon the poles of its ancient routine.

In the winter when I cannot work with, or study, the bees themselves I have enjoyed collecting old books on bees and beekeeping: and I have delighted in corresponding with beekeepers who are as besotted as I am in their interest in the lore of the bee. I have had marvelously good letters from men I have never seen, both in this country and in England—even from China! Through the years I have managed to collect most of the early English and American books dealing with the subject, besides some in foreign languages. It is a vast and interesting literature, to which some of the world's greatest writers have delighted to contribute. What youngster in college has not heard of Vergil's book —the fourth *Georgic*—which accepts the strangest superstitions and tells for truth the wildest nonsense regarding the honeybee? I have myself the earliest English book on the subject, that of John Hyll, printed in 1565, which Shakespeare himself might have read. Hyll cribbed unmercifully from earlier writers, especially Vergil and Columella, as they in their turn cribbed from the Greeks, but he did much to open English eyes to the wonders of the bee people.

I have had so many adventures in collecting these old books that I should like one day to write them down. What ancient bee enthusiasts have I talked with, what tramps I have taken in America and in England, poking around in dusty attics and crowded cellars of old bookshops in London and Edinburgh and Bristol, to say nothing of Paris: what curious and interesting people have I met, and while I am far from having all the old books on the subject that I covet (some are too costly for me) I have many of the best and most interesting, including a number of excellent first editions, from the sixteenth century downward. But all this I must leave for later consideration—say from my hundredth year onward!

I never knew an evil yet cured by mere opposition.

Looking back over yesterday, what did I do? I talked too much: was silent too little. One never regrets what he did not say.

FEBRUARY 27. Rain all day long—warm, drifting rain, full of the feeling of the south, almost springlike. I was busy with my writing for as many hours as I could stand.

The rain did not keep me from a long tramp with a free mind, a contented spirit, and muddy legs. I stay my haste, I make delays.

Wherein men differ most is in the power of *seeing*. I mean seeing with all that goes with it and is implicit in it. Seeing lies at the foundation of all science and all art. He who sees most knows most, lives most, enjoys most.

So many people see nothing whatever, freshly, for themselves.

MARCH

IN THE COUNTRYMAN'S YEAR

"A private Life is to be preferred; the Honour and Gain of publick Posts bearing no proportion with the Comfort of it. The one is free *and* quiet, *the other* servile *and* noisy."—From WILLIAM PENN'S MAXIMS.

CHAPTER XII

MARCH IN THE COUNTRYMAN'S YEAR

MARCH 6. A remarkable springlike day, full
of sunshine and running water—and a soft
blue haze in the south—and a hungry unrest
of the spirit. I could not think of work, but
of the sap running in maple trees, and the
meadows coming bare, and the young things
of the woods peeping out to see if winter is
over and gone. I think I never saw the sky
so high and clear, or ever knew the wind so
sweet.

I knew it was only false spring at best, and

that winter had not yet surrendered, but I
walked out through my orchard looking nar-
rowly at every tree, I studied the peach buds,
I stood long before the winter hives listening
to the eager bees, they too out for a flight in
the sunshine. I looked hopefully in the grass
where the crocuses are planted—and, with a
longing I cannot describe, followed the flight
of crows high across the barren fields. I saw a
flock of sparrows among the bushes, flitting
about with a kind of lively, fearless excitement, and it so touched something within me
that it seemed to me I liked them as I never
had before. It came to me there on the hillside that I knew why it was that St Francis so
loved the larks of Assisi. I remembered dimly
how he had wished that the Emperor might
forever protect them; and this recollection
was so hauntingly pleasant to me that when
I came in, at length, to my study I looked in
The Little Flowers and found the passage
(Chapter CXIV) wherein St Francis is
quoted:

"If I were to speak to the Emperor I
would, supplicating and persuading him, tell
him for the love of God and me to make a
special law that no man should take or kill

sister Larks nor do them any harm. Likewise
that all the Podestas of the towns and the
Lords of castles and villages should be bound
every year on Christmas Day to counsel men
to throw wheat and other grains outside the
cities and castles, that our sister Larks may
have something to eat, and also the other
birds, on a day of such solemnity."

So it was, upon reading this passage, that
my mind went pleasantly and humorously
away with me, and I thought of asking the
President of the United States and the Governor of Massachusetts (God bless our Com-
monwealth!) and our village Selectman (in
his white apron with his cleaver in his hand
—for he is our butcher) that they deal well
by sister sparrow "and also the other birds"—
including the stately pheasants which stride
often among our trees and are heedlessly
slaughtered in the fall—and that in these
cold and wintry days of March, they throw
wheat and other grain upon Amity street so
that sister sparrow may have something to
eat. And I thought how amused the President
would be, and the Governor, and our Selectman, with his cleaver, and how full of surprise, if I should go to them with such an odd

suggestion when they were thinking solemnly of matters they considered of far greater importance.

It seems to me I have had much joy of this day, and many pleasant thoughts. And I have not worked at all, and am not sorry, either; for there are days when it is well that a man should let the quiet of nature completely fill his soul.

Is it true as Walt Whitman has said?—

"There will never be any more perfection than there is now,
Nor any more heaven or hell than there is now."

If it is true, how important—of all things —to learn how to live now.

MARCH 9. It is never far to the unfamiliar; at any moment the wild, the eerie, the mysterious may ruffle the stagnant pool of our mediocre days.

This morning early we heard strange sounds, wild lost cries, in the field below us. All the earth was cloaked in fog, a hushed and unfamiliar world. I tiptoed down through the garden and orchard. Every moment the cries grew wilder and lonelier. At length I saw through the thick fog moving shapes in the field, ghostly large in the dim light, like a visitation from another planet. I felt at first a literal shudder of astonishment —for in all my years in the country I had never before seen anything like it. A flock of stately white wild geese had settled in our meadow—lost in the fog. I came within a stone's throw of them before they saw me and rose in clamorous alarm, their powerful wings soon lifting them into the mystery and silence of the sky.

Strangely, all day, the experience has lingered warm in my mind. I have thought of the wild geese flying tirelessly northward through the cold Canadian skies and, though befogged for a day, pressing onward to the north—something wild and free and mysterious—and beautiful.

MARCH 10. I tramped the muddy roads, downward through the marshes, four or five miles. Much snow left. I hoped to see some of the early birds, but, save for crows, starlings and a few song sparrows, I saw nothing except a small hawk perched upon the top of a dead stub. The brook was turgid and muddy, the sky overcast and leaden, and all the landscape sad and gray. The distant hills, streaked with snow, looked like bearded old men.

Still pools in old woods, full of leaves, mirrors of heaven.

"We cling to this strange thing that shines in the sunlight, and are sick with love for it, because we have not seen beyond the veil."

MARCH 11. A real spring day, with the snow melting and the sun warm on my shoulder blades as I walked. I heard the crows and the jays calling.

Just at evening, as I passed, I looked in on a camp of woodchoppers, rough, bewhiskered men with weather-bronzed faces. To my amazement they were sitting around their little red-hot stove listening to the radio. I heard the strains of it before I reached their hut. In the old days, not so long ago, what dull evenings—pipes and cards and the endless boredom of their own talk—now they can, if they like, hear Kreisler play, or Galli-Curci sing, or the President explain his poli-

cies. *If they like!* But will they like? Here
again a miracle of science, a prodigy of invention—will men use it for the greatest
things it offers, or the worst? Will they get
out of it in enlargement anything they cannot
themselves put into it in understanding? How
inevitably, after all, everything gets back to
the man himself.

Tranquillity is an achievement; back of
tranquillity lies always conquered unhappiness. Placidity may be only bovine.

MARCH 14. Heavy rain. We are wandering
between two worlds, one dead, the other pow-
erless to be born. Yesterday we had intimations of spring; today nature has lost heart,
weeps at its own futility.

Hard at my laborious writing.

Again in the orchard, pruning my apple
trees. They have now grown so large that the
task is considerable. I can perch in the top
branches of trees I myself planted only a few
years ago. Until the last season or so, no one
ever pruned, fertilized, or sprayed these trees
but me.

A day of easy joy.

"Is it nothing to you, all ye that pass by?"

So in my deep mood would I be crying at every roadside, upon every hill, in every town. For how can one look upon this world, made cruel by men, without asking all who pass by to look at it and make it better?

"Everywhere," I read in Goethe, "men learn only from men and things they love"— a saying I think everlastingly true. It grows upon one, with clearer understanding, as he lives and thinks.

MARCH 18. Walked uptown. So many interesting thoughts crowded upon me that I was happy.

Saintsbury says that the most beautiful English prose is in Chapter VIII of the Song of Solomon: today in an essay I have been reading I find that Paul Bourget considers a passage wherein Pascal "affirms our human dignity" "among the most beautiful, if not absolutely the most beautiful" lines ever traced by the hand of man. High praise! Here is the paragraph he quotes:

"Man is nothing but a reed, the weakest thing of nature, but he is a reed that thinks.

The universe need not arm itself to stamp
him out. A vapor, a drop of water, suffices to
slay him, but even at the moment when the
universe stamps him out man is still nobler
than that which slays him, because he knows
that it is slaying, and the universe knows nothing—not even its superior strength."

MARCH 22. True spring day. Snow all gone
here in the valley: a little remains in the
Whately hills, and now and then an old worn
icy heap north of clumps of pines. Even the
frost is mostly out of the ground, though I
found a little six or eight inches down when
I tried to dig out some spring parsnips. It is
good to be out. I worked this afternoon gathering up and burning the prunings from the
orchard. The bees were lively and actually
seemed to be getting a little nectar from the
lowly chickweed, which here and there, in the
garden, has begun to blossom.

Most of the day I was hard at work at my
desk.

M—— has been tearing down the ancient
rail fence I loved to walk beside. It skirted
his wood lot and in spring grew full of cherry

trees, and vines upon it, and here and there, pushing sturdily upward, young pines and hemlocks. Progress! Progress! In its precious place he has set out red angle-iron posts, hard, sharp, efficient, and strung barbed wire upon them. He gains six or eight feet of arable land along his field wherein he will raise corn and potatoes. But I shall not again go that way when the cherry trees come to blossom and the wild grapes in May fill all the air with their fragrance.

MARCH 23. Just at evening I heard from outside my study window a sound for which I have been eagerly listening for a week or more. I rushed out, and sure enough, a robin flew across the lawn and into the thicket. It is the first I have heard or seen this year, although neighbors have been reporting them for several days; and in former years I have seen them as early as March 11.

A delightful moment of suspense—the moment at the telephone after the operator has told you that someone is calling you from "long distance"—the swift, eager review of friends, one of whom may be on the other end of the line, whose voice will soon come to your ear.

MARCH 25. Our friends having invited us to visit their sugarbush, we drove to Sunderland and walked three miles up Mount Toby. The wood roads were heavy with mud, with here and there patches of old snow: scarcely a sign of spring except the running sap and the swelling willow buds.

Hubbard's bush is in a rocky field on the flank of the mountain—an ancient wooden shack standing among magnificent old maple trees. When we came first in sight of it, it looked as though it were on fire, for the steam from the boiling sap was pouring out through every crack. It was indeed a stirring place—men and boys hallooing in the woods as they chopped fuel for the fire, or drove the sledges down the mountainside with barrels of sap, or ran in and out of the sugarhouse. As we came nearer we caught the ambrosial odor of the steaming syrup, and a moment later we were welcomed by Hubbard and his boys.

It was a perfect sugar day. Last night it froze hard, and today the sun shines warm: and every one of the hundreds of trees that have been tapped are dripping sap into the shining pails that hang from the spiles.

The sap is boiled in long shallow pans heated by a roaring fire of four-foot wood, there being a gradual flow from the pan where the sap comes in from the vat to the deeper pan where the syrup begins to grow thick and is of a deep golden color.

Hubbard is an expert—he is of the third generation of a family that has made sugar every spring for seventy years there upon the flanks of Toby—he knows by trial with a ladle when the syrup "aprons off" or "hairs off" whether it is ready to pour into the cans to sell as syrup or to boil down still further into sugar. We brought in pails and pans of snow to "sugar off" and ate our luncheon on a board table at one side of the saphouse. Afterwards, sitting by the steaming pans, there was mighty joking and storytelling.

Hubbard told me that a few of the prize maples in his bush are so large that they will produce three or four barrels of sap in a season. Each barrel will boil down to about a gallon of syrup: that is, each of these great trees will produce three and a half gallons of syrup, selling this year for about $2.50 or $3.00—say $10 to a tree. Or, if the process is continued and sugar is produced, we have these results: a gallon of syrup weighing eleven pounds will boil down to make some eight pounds of sugar, selling at fifty or sixty cents a pound. The farmers here say there is "no real money in it"; but sugar making comes at a time of the year when ordinary farm work is slack (it will be ten days yet before they begin to put out their tobacco frames), and some of them say frankly that the spring makes them restless and they want to get into the woods and see the sap running. The fact is, they enjoy it.

MARCH 28. It was windy and raw, but I found, under the grape arbor, the first snowdrops beginning to blossom. Grass on southern slopes shows green. I am impatient for the spring.

It is no excuse—turning from reason because the mass of men are not moved by it.

Nature ripens the fruit first on the broken stem. But it is poor fruit.

A man cannot think chiefly of himself without being discouraged.

MARCH 29. I put up my cold frame and spread manure on the asparagus bed. It has been a long, cold winter.

What is the greatest moment of the week in a country town?

I know: Saturday forenoon about half past eleven. Walk up Pleasant Street with me and look at all the prosperous merchants hurrying to the bank with their week-end deposits. How rich we are! Here is Mr F—— with his in an old, well-thumbed cigar box, and Mr H——, without his overcoat, tiptoeing along the icy walk, looking rather chilly—for he is running out of his overheated store—but energetic and confident, with a roll of bills in one hand half the size of a stovepipe, and a canvas bag in the other full of coin. We exhibit our money in public only upon such hallowed occasions as this. In the bank you will find Mr A——, the contractor, at the desk making up his weekly pay roll, with money all around him: and Mr M——, the mason, with his worn moneybag, hurrying out to pay off his men. Money travels Saturday morning! If you would know how rich we are and prosperous and contented—making believe we are not in the least excited—just travel with me up Pleasant Street at half past eleven on Saturday morning.

MARCH 30. Today, in the marshes, I saw the first of the skunk cabbages thrusting their way upward from the sedgy brookside. I have seen them thus every spring nearly all the years of my life. There was nothing strange or newly beautiful about them. I did not care to look closely at them or to handle them, much less to smell them, and yet those cowled heads rising from the slime of the marsh, seeking the sunshine of spring, gave me such a thrill as I cannot describe. It seemed suddenly and greatly beautiful to me, the patience of nature. Going on, going on! The cheerful continuity of birth and growth. Whatever happens, it endures: year after year for inconceivable millions of years: and never discouraged!

So I walked, and my heart went out to the old friends, the old simple things, of the woods and the hills. That riveter of the forest, Master Woodpecker, I stopped long to watch among the trees, and Swooper Robin flashing across the sunny open spaces. Trill-leader Sparrow was there in the thicket, four wild ducks splashed upward from the marshy swale, lifting into the high still air. Old Gray Woodchuck, wearying of winter, had ventured out to sit in the sun. I stood long on the brookside watching a number of lubberly chub balancing themselves against the current in the depths of the sunny water.

I came across today some lines in Epictetus which express one of the prime difficulties of life—that is, for a man to act always upon a clear central principle, determined by him as inevitable to his own nature and character:

"You must know," says Epictetus, "that it is no easy thing for a principle to become a man's own, unless each day he maintain it and hear it maintained, as well as work it out in life."

So true this is! It requires that a man shall never relax from the thing he holds to be true: so that, as he grows older, any problem, or trouble, or sorrow will not overwhelm him, but meet instantly the solvent of principles which he has established and accepted. We attain tranquillity by no sudden adoption or conversion: most precious of possessions, it is a living thing, with its roots deep in the soil of our nature or character.

MARCH 31. Yesterday in the hills I returned to my youth and made me a butternut whistle.

When I was a boy I loved well, in spring, to make whistles out of the smooth branches of the butternut tree. It was in those first delicious early days of the year when the sap had begun to flow, and the crows were crying in the old woods, and the skunk cabbage was pushing its hooded head up through the rich green mosses of the swamps.

I cut a fair young branch and whittled one end down for a mouthpiece. Then I made a notch at just the right distance for a stop, and then, a few inches further down, I cut a circular ring around the branch, the length my whistle was to be. I wet all the bark with my tongue and, taking my knife by the blade end, I rapped on the bark to loosen it, using my knee for an anvil. I continued for a long time this patient, gentle rapping until I had covered every spot upon the surface of my whistle. Then the great moment came! Would it peel? I took the stick in both hands and twisted the end that was to form the whistle. I can remember yet the thrill I always had when the bark slipped on the wood and I could draw it off whole, leaving the glistening white core underneath. If it split in the process, woe was me: I had to begin all over again. But when it peeled perfectly I hollowed out the wood to make the resonant hollow for the whistle and cut with care the thin space from the mouthpiece down to the stop. Then I slipped the bark back on again. With what expectancy I now put it to my lips: what joy I knew when it gave out the first thin clear notes! I remember well lying back among the brown leaves of a certain hillside, closing my eyes, and blowing with a kind of ecstasy upon my butternut whistle.

Yesterday I made me a whistle exactly like that of my boyhood—but where was the ecstasy when I blew it?

David Grayson was the pen name of accomplished turn of the century journalist Ray Stannard Baker. From the March day in 1894 when Baker set out to follow Coxey's Army for the Chicago *Record*, he became an American chronicler. "When I really enjoyed an experience, when I saw or heard something which struck me as wonderful, when I met a man or a woman who interested me, whom I deeply admired or loved, I could not let these things go by with a glance...Of all the ways ever I found for squeezing the last savor from an experience, the best is to write about it..."

Baker had a long, productive relationship with the prestigious *McClure's Magazine*, bringing to its pages portraits of some of the day's geniuses: Theodore Roosevelt, Joel Chandler Harris, Stephen Crane, Admiral Dewey, Thomas Alva Edison, Guglielmo Marconi... At a political gathering in January, 1910, he was enlightened with a speech by the president of Princeton University. "Here, it seemed, was the magical touch of great leadership: the touch of courage. Was (this man) after all really available as a national leader?" Thus began the close friendship of Ray Stannard Baker and Woodrow Wilson, Baker following the future president throughout his administration and ultimately to Europe in 1918, where he organized the press department at the Paris Peace Conference and reported the long, often bitter controversies over the League of Nations. Baker became Woodrow Wilson's official biographer and was awarded the Pulitzer Prize for his seven-volume *Woodrow Wilson: Life and Letters.*

But Ray Stannard Baker was a lover of quiet ways and simple pleasures, goals not easily attained in the hectic journalistic world. Thus emerged David Grayson, the writer in Baker who "wished most, if it can be expressed in a phrase, to be an introducer of human beings to one another, to be a maker of understandings." In pursuit of a more rational lifestyle, he moved his family to Amherst, Massachusetts, where they built their quiet, country dream home. "Every tree, every shrub, every berry bush around the house and in the garden we planted with our own hands." From his Amherst refuge, Grayson recorded his daily thoughts and observations on the state of the farm, his neighbors, his bees, the nation and mankind.